The Complete Guide to

Welsh Terriers

Cathleen Peters Saito

LP Media Inc. Publishing
Text copyright © 2023 by LP Media Inc.
All rights reserved.

No part of this book may be reproduced or transmitted in any form or by any means, electronic or mechanical, including photocopying, recording, or by an information storage and retrieval system – except by a reviewer who may quote brief passages in a review to be printed in a magazine or newspaper – without permission in writing from the publisher. For information address LP Media Inc. Publishing, 1405 Kingsview Ln N, Plymouth, MN 55447

www.lpmedia.org

Publication Data

Cathleen Peters Saito
The Complete Guide to Welsh Terriers – First edition.
Summary: "Successfully raising a Welsh Terrier from puppy to old age"
Provided by publisher.
ISBN: 978-1-954288-76-8
[1. The Complete Guide to Welsh Terriers – Non-Fiction] I. Title.

This book has been written with the published intent to provide accurate and authoritative information in regard to the subject matter included. While every reasonable precaution has been taken in preparation of this book the author and publisher expressly disclaim responsibility for any errors, omissions, or adverse effects arising from the use or application of the information contained inside. The techniques and suggestions are to be used at the reader's discretion and are not to be considered a substitute for professional veterinary care. If you suspect a medical problem with your dog, consult your veterinarian.

Design by Sorin Rădulescu
First hardcover edition, 2023

Table of Contents

Acknowledgments 1

Chapter 1
History and Description 3
Introduction 3
Welsh Terrier History 5
Physical Characteristics 8
Welsh Terrier Temperament and Behavior 12
Is a Welsh Terrier a Good Fit for You? 17

Chapter 2
Life Stages of the Welsh Terrier 19
The Puppy 19
The Adolescent 23
The Adult 25
The Senior 26

Chapter 3
Choosing a Welsh Terrier 29
Buying vs. Adopting 29
Age and Sex Considerations 30
Finding a Responsible Breeder 32
Communicating with Your Breeder 35

Health Tests and Certifications and Questions 38
Tips for Picking Your Puppy 40
Researching Rescues 41
Tips for Adopting a Welsh Terrier 44

Chapter 4
Preparing for Your Welsh Terrier 45
Getting Your Children and Current Pets Ready 46
Preparing Your Home 48
A Safe Space for Your Dog 49
Preparing Outside Spaces 49
Get the Essentials 53
Nutrition 55
Choosing a Vet & Other Professionals 59

Chapter 5
Bringing Home Your Welsh Terrier 61
The Importance of Having a Plan 61
Introducing Your Human Family 64
If There Is Already Another Dog at Home 65
Introducing Your Cat 68
The First Night 70
First Vet Visit 72
Puppy Classes 74
Toy Safety 75

Chapter 6
House-training Your Welsh Terrier 77
The Importance of Routine..77
Supervision during House-training...78
Positive Reinforcement 80
Where a Dog Goes Potty 81
The Puppy 82
The Adult..84
Marking 85
Potty on Command..86
Pee Pads and Other Indoor Potty Alternatives 87
Crate Training...88

Chapter 7
Grooming Your Welsh Terrier 91
The Welsh Terrier Coat..91
Brushing..91
Stripping vs. Clipping..93
Bathing 99
Nails.. 101
Ears... 102
Eyes... 104
Doggy Dental Care 105
Final Thoughts on Grooming... 106

Chapter 8
Health Care 107
Vaccinations.. 107
Internal and External Parasites 109
How to Help Your Welsh Terrier Live Longer 111
Welsh Terrier Health Problems..................................... 113
Is It an Emergency? 118
First Aid 119
Pet Insurance... 120

Chapter 9
Building Confidence and Making Friends—Human & Canine 121
Why Early Socialization Is Important 122
Tips for Socializing Your Puppy 123
Teaching Your Dog How to Greet People 125
Introducing Your Welsh Terrier to Other People's Dogs.. 126
Welsh Terriers and Small Children 128
Being a Good Neighbor... 131
Dog Laws.. 132

Chapter 10
Training 133
The Benefits of Proper Training 136
Taking Classes/Lessons vs. Sending Your Welshie to a Trainer 137

Choosing a Trainer 138
Practice Matters 140
Behave Yourself 140
Training Tips 142

Chapter 11
Basic Lessons 145
May I Have Your Attention, Please? 146
Coming When Called 147
Sit and Release 150
Walking On-leash 153
Stand 156
Down 156
Stay 157
Leave It 158
Drop It 160
Tricks 160

Chapter 12
Behavioral Issues 161
Living with a Teenage Welsh Terrier 162
Chewing 163
Biting 164
Growling: Listen, Don't Scold 166
Resource Guarding 166
The Incorrigible People-Jumper 168

Barking 169
Digging 171
Separation Anxiety... 171
When You Need Help 172
If You Don't Want or Can't Keep Your Welsh Terrier 173

Chapter 13
Traveling with Your Welsh Terrier 175
Planning Your Trip 176
Dog Crates and Other Restraints.. 177
Preparing Your Welsh Terrier for the Trip 180
Packing for Your Dog 182
Travel Tips 183
When You Can't Take Your Dog on a Trip 185

Chapter 14
Activities for Welsh Terriers 187
Faux Hunting Games 188
Companion Activities.. 198
Speedy Dog Sports 203
The Nose Knows 208
Have Fun and Make Friends as Your Dog Earns
Accolades 208

Chapter 15
The Senior Welsh Terrier 209
Basics of Senior Dog Care 209
Helping Your Dog Adapt to Old Age 211
End of Life 213
Grieving the Loss of Your Pet 215

Chapter 16
Resources for Welsh Terrier Owners 217
Health 217
End of Life 218
Travel 219
Dog Tricks 219
Earthdog and Ratting 219
Companion Dog Activities 220
Lure Coursing/Terrier Racing 220
Flyball 220
Agility 221
Nose Work 221
Training 221
Books & Magazines 222

Acknowledgments

A lot of talented people—in and out of the dog world—contributed to this book. I want to thank Diane Amendola and Bruce Benderson for their encouragement and support during the creation of this book. I am also grateful to Steve Ambrosio, Ashbey Photography, Lucy Bailey, Diane Bauman, Linda Brisbin, Rhonda Cassidy, Mary Duafala, DiAnn Flory, Lyn Hollis, Frankie Joiris, Katie Cane, Sari Mäkälä, John Melair, Hiroshi Saito, Max Searls, Jill See, and Addison Thompson for the quoted material and photography they supplied me with.

Acknowledgments

CHAPTER 1

History and Description

Introduction

The Welsh Terrier is an outgoing, energetic, and friendly medium-sized dog. The average life span for the terriers, affectionately called Welshies, is 12 to 15 years.

This ancient breed from Wales was originally bred to control rats and other vermin on farms and hunt foxes, badgers, and otters in underground dens and rock formations. They were developed by rural people who toiled to make a living on the Welsh land—not the aristocracy.

Today, the Welsh Terrier is among the At Watch breeds on the United Kingdom's Kennel Club (KC) list of native breeds in danger of disappearing. Dog breeds that originated in the UK and have fewer than 300 KC registrations per year are listed as Vulnerable. Those with 300 to 450 KC registrations per year, such as the Welsh Terrier, are listed as At Watch.

Though its numbers are generally small, this breed can be found in many countries around the world. The first recorded import of Welsh Terriers into the United States occurred in 1886, and the Welsh Terrier Club of America was formed in 1900. In the 1960s, John F. Kennedy had a Welsh Terrier named Charlie in the White House.

While the modern Welsh Terrier is primarily a show dog and pet, the traits that made it a specialized hunter centuries ago are still strong in the breed. Understanding the working history and traits of this breed is the key to comprehending the current generation and forming a good relationship with individual dogs.

Chapter 1: History and Description

Photo Courtesy of Katarína Franková

My second Welsh Terrier, Champion Rubicon's Sugar Bear, taught me the importance of the working instincts in the breed. This beautiful black and tan dog came into my life after he retired from a successful career in the show ring.

Months after we got him, I saw a flyer for an upcoming American Working Terrier Association (AWTA) den trial: a test in an artificial underground tunnel of a terrier's (or Dachshund's) natural working instinct. It was nearby, so my husband and I packed the car and headed to our first AWTA trial with Bear. We failed the test that day because my dog took too long to get to the end of the tunnel, but after it, Bear was happier than I had ever seen him.

That day I realized the importance of the working instinct in Welsh Terriers. It started my quest to learn more about their prey-driven behaviors and led to many wonderful adventures for me with Bear.

Welsh Terriers were originally bred to do a job, and to this day, they crave working for their owners. Understanding and utilizing the ancient hunting instincts still deeply embedded in this breed can make training them much easier and life with them a joy. Trying to ignore or squelch these traits can only serve to make the lives of both dog and owner difficult.

Welsh Terrier History

The name of this breed tells its history. The term "terrier" derives from the Latin word "terra," which means earth. Terriers are hunting dogs that originally specialized in digging for small game and pursuing quarry underground. The "Welsh" part of the name denotes Wales as the area where this particular working terrier was developed. As early as the 10th century, small working terriers may have helped farmers in the British Isles protect their land from vermin such as mice, rats, foxes, and badgers. They also would have been useful for hunting rabbits.

The exact origin of Welsh Terriers is not known. Some people argue the breed descends from the Old English Black and Tan Terrier. But others believe the Welsh Terrier is ancestor to the many types of black and tan terriers found throughout the British Isles. However, the truth has been obscured over the centuries. I. Morlais Thomas, author of *The Welsh Terrier Handbook* in 1959, questioned why the people of Wales wouldn't have developed their own Welsh Terrier to hunt the abundant vermin in that country. He points out that the people of Wales developed their own Welsh Pony, Welsh Black Cattle, and a number of Welsh dog breeds, including the Welsh Springer Spaniel and Welsh Hound. So why not their own Welsh Terrier?

The first mention of a black and tan terrier, possibly the Welsh Terrier, in literature was made by a Welsh poet in 1450. It mentions a gift of "...a good black and red terrier bitch, to throttle the brown polecat and to tear up the red fox."

In the early days of the breed, Welsh Terriers were valued for their working abilities and not for their looks. The dogs had to be confident and brave enough to face a foe in dark and unfamiliar spaces underground and agile and energetic enough to scamper over rocky terrain and work in narrow tunnels. When hunting otters, working terriers had to be able to swim because the entrance to an otter's riverbank den was sometimes underwater.

Welsh Terriers used all their senses in the hunt for foxes, otters, and badgers below ground and rats and rabbits above ground. They also needed to be smart and resourceful enough not to be killed by their quarry. After a hard day's work, these dogs were good-tempered enough to enjoy the warmth of their owner's hearth with the family. The early Welsh Terrier also hunted with hounds and had to be calm and sociable to work with the packs. These little dogs also needed the stamina to run with hounds and a strong constitution to survive the elements.

> **DID YOU KNOW?**
>
> **The Welsh Terrier Club of America (WTCA)**
>
> Founded in 1900, the Welsh Terrier Club of America (WTCA) is this breed's American Kennel Club (AKC) parent club. From annual conformation shows to quarterly newsletters, the WTCA strives to educate dog owners and the public about responsible ownership, health, and standards of the Welsh Terrier. Members of the WTCA must be sponsored by two members in good standing and sign a code of ethics upon acceptance. For more information about becoming a WTCA or the club's annual shows, visit www.welshterrier.org.

Welsh Terriers barked and nipped at their quarry to make it leave its subterranean refuge and go above ground to the waiting hunter, or they made enough noise beneath the earth for hunters to dig to them. When the animal couldn't be bolted or dug, these terriers were expected to make a kill in the earth. The Welsh fox was considered so fierce that some hunters would send two or three Welsh Terriers down a hole at the same time to dispatch it. The traits of confidence, gameness, intelligence, energy, sociability, and calmness were so strongly bred into early working Welsh Terriers that these characteristics continue in the breed today.

Understanding this working history is key to understanding and developing the best possible relationship with individual Welsh Terriers. In the early days of the breed, pedigrees were not kept. The best working dogs were bred to the best working bitches.

The Kennel Club of England did not exist until 1873. Before that time, early dog shows took place at agricultural events, with Welsh Terriers being shown in classes like the Working Terrier class. The first show with separate classes for Welsh Terriers was held in Wales in 1884.

Starting in the 1850s, there was a dispute between two factions as to whether the breed was actually the Old English Black and Tan Terrier (OEBTT) or the Welsh Terrier. The Kennel Club recognized classes for both terriers starting in 1885. The Welsh Terrier prevailed and continued on its new path to show dog stardom in 1887, when the Kennel Club ended classes for the OEBTT.

The first champion Welsh Terriers looked a bit different from today's Welshie. As people began to realize the value of champion show dogs, more emphasis was placed on physical beauty by the breeders. Over the years, the head of the Welsh Terrier has become a little longer, the furnishings (hair on the face and legs) and coat have become more plentiful, and some modern dogs may have chests that are too big for their original work below ground in Wales.

The chest of a working terrier should be spannable by an average man's hand if that dog is the right size to work quarry underground. To span a dog, the hands are placed around its chest behind its elbows, with fingers touching. The thumbs should slightly overlap on top of the spine as the dog's front legs are lifted slightly off the ground. This is a measurement long used by people who hunt their terriers in the earth; it is not used for modern Welshies in the show ring.

During World War I, the courage, tenacity, stamina, and trainability of the Welsh Terrier helped them succeed as messenger dogs for Great Britain's army. In the midst of heavy bombardments, when telephone communications were near impossible and human runners too risky, these dogs braved smoke, noise, shell holes, vehicle traffic, corpses, muddy terrain, and even poisonous gas to carry important messages between the front lines and headquarters.

I personally witnessed the tenacity of a Welsh Terrier to overcome all obstacles when performing a job at an AWTA den trial held after a torrential rainstorm. The ground was saturated, and there was up to an inch of water in some parts of the artificial tunnel.

Qualifying dogs that are fastest to reach the rats are given awards at AWTA trials. In my experience, small Jack Russell-type Terriers usually win the top prize. But on this day, when most dogs were cautious in the mud and water, my Welshie paid no heed to those conditions and put all the other dogs to shame as she crawled at high speed through the mud and water to reach the tunnel's end.

In some European countries, the breed is still used for hunting above and below ground. And while Welsh Terriers are not often used for hunting in the United States today, they still retain the character traits that once made them good hunters in Wales. These working qualities have helped these dogs find success in new jobs.

Nowadays, the Welsh Terrier is an accomplished show dog and cherished pet. The breed has produced show champions in many countries and won numerous Best-In-Show awards around the world. Outside of the ring, these dogs add a spark of joy to the lives of their owners.

In addition to the show ring, the modern Welsh Terrier has found success in the agility ring. Finnish Welsh Terrier Dirty Harry (FI Ch C.I.A. FI & SE & NO AgCh Vicway Dirty Harry), bred by Sari Mäkelä, was the FCI Individual Agility World Champion in his height category in 1999. Today, many Welsh Terriers and their owners enjoy competing in agility rings around the world. Welsh Terriers in the United States also currently participate in obedience, freestyle, trick dog, tracking, and artificial den trials, as well as in therapy dog visits and other events.

Physical Characteristics

The Welsh Terrier is a good fit for those looking for physical characteristics such as small and sturdy, with a medium-length wiry coat that does not shed much. In some ways, the Welsh Terrier is a very 'average' dog; its physical characteristics are not extreme in ways that other breeds may be. It is not very large or very small, very longhaired or very shorthaired, very long-backed or very short-legged, extra-short-nosed or extra-long-eared, very wrinkly, or very drooly.

LUCY BAILEY
WYSIWYG Welsh Terriers

GChS Abbyrose Black Diamond in show groom

The Welsh Terrier of today has been smartened up over the years for the show ring. However, it is still a rugged-looking, medium-sized dog.

My dog Bear was a striking creature to behold. Having been successful in the show ring, he had a medium-sized body that was sturdy and well-balanced. He exuded power, confidence, and joy on our daily walks, and people often stopped to meet him and compliment his good looks. Both men and women thought him a very attractive dog.

Welsh Terriers aren't flashy or fancy. Nor are they coarse. The Welsh Terrier's appearance is one of moderation and balanced parts. Their solid, compact bodies, brick-shaped heads, and wiry coats give them a workmanlike appearance that is fitting for a dog that originally belonged to the common man.

The Welsh Terrier is described as a square dog, meaning it's as tall as it is long, with a rectangular-shaped head. Males generally stand about 15 to 15 1/2 inches tall at the withers (the bony protrusion that is the top of the shoulders between the neck and back) and have an average weight of 20 pounds. Bitches tend to be a little smaller. Of course, there is variation in size, with some Welsh being larger or smaller than the average.

The planes of the Welsh head are level, and the foreface should be the same length as the forehead. The strong muzzle is only slightly narrower than the back skull. The cheeks are a little more muscular than the Wire Fox Terrier. Between the ears, the Welsh head is flat and slightly wider than the Fox Terrier. Just below the forehead, the Welsh have a very slight stop, the area where the muzzle meets the skull at a longitudinal angle, between small, almond-shaped, dark brown eyes. This terrier's eyes are well set in the skull, placed a fair distance apart, and very expressive.

The small V-shaped ears of the Welsh Terrier fold just above the skull to fall forward near the outside corner of the eye when they are relaxed. Welsh Terriers can move their ears slightly up and forward when they are attentive. These folded ears would have protected the original working Welsh Terriers' ears from dirt as they hunted underground.

Traditionally, the furnishings (whiskers and eyebrows) on the face are groomed so that the outline of the head resembles a brick. From the head, a moderately long, thick neck with a slight arch descends gently into long, sloping shoulders.

Welsh Terriers have what is termed a straight front, or terrier front. If you observe the dog's body in side profile, the point of the shoulder is level with the fore chest. This means that the shoulder does not protrude past the front of the chest. This does not mean that the shoulders, from the front point to the highest point, are upright. They still need to lie back with good angulation for the dog to have an adequate stride.

The Welsh Terrier's straight front evolved for its original work digging quarry in the earth. For this construction, the upper arm is slightly shorter than the shoulder. This ensures that the dog's elbows are not impeded by the deepest part of the chest when crawling and digging through tunnels. Their front legs are straight like columns with toes pointing forward. It's a front-end assembly that makes for a very powerful digger when the dog is navigating a fox or badger den.

The topline of the Welsh is level, and the top of its head should be about the same height as the top of the docked tail. (An undocked tail

Honeypaw's Super Nova

might be about an inch or so longer.) In the United States, Welsh tails are docked. This has long been the tradition in the breed. But as more countries have banned tail docking, some Welsh Terriers are appearing in the United States with unmodified tails. These tails are sturdy and set high on the back.

A solid tail was important for these dogs' original work underground because it provided hunters with a solid handle for pulling the dogs out of the earth when necessary. A healthy Welsh Terrier will carry its tail in an upright and confident manner.

A Welsh Terrier's hindquarters are strong and muscular. They should have good drive from behind, but the stride of the rear legs should not be longer than that of the front legs. The movement of the Welsh Terrier is balanced, workmanlike, and ground-covering. It is not an up-and-down prance or an extremely long and floating stride.

Welsh Terriers belong to a double-coated breed. That means the Welsh Terrier has a soft, short undercoat for insulation and a close-fitting thick and wiry topcoat for protection from rain, wind, and dirt. The furnishings on the head and legs are, in the best of cases, dense and wiry. This dog rarely sheds if brushed and combed at least once a week and clipped or hand-stripped several times a year. In fact, if regularly brushed, most Welshies do not require frequent bathing. They may only need a bath a couple of times a year except in certain situations, such as when the dog rolls in mud or in something stinky.

My terrier, Bear, had a red "tan" on his head, underbelly, butt, and legs that was set off beautifully by a jet-black jacket and undercoat on his back. This ebony color spread along his neck and the top of his tail and into his upper thighs. He had a few white hairs interspersed with the black hairs of his jacket, which were nice proof for dog show judges that he was not artificially colored.

The Welsh Terrier head, underbelly, butt, and legs are a tan that can range from deep red to slightly lighter shades. Their jackets can be black or grizzle (a black and tan-blended color). Born mostly black, the color of Welsh Terrier puppies gradually changes during their first year so that the head, legs, underbelly, and butt become tan while the jacket stays black or changes to grizzle. Their nose and lips remain black, as do the pads of their feet and their toenails.

Welsh Terrier Temperament and Behavior

> *Welshies are typically very active, curious, and intelligent dogs. They enjoy being involved in whatever you are doing. If they get bored, they will usually seek entertainment for themselves—this can be good or bad! They should be indoor dogs, but with a securely fenced backyard to run off energy and safely chase after squirrels.*
>
> ELIZABETH BERRY
> *Airedale and Welsh Terrier Rescue*

Genetics and early socialization influence temperament and behavior. Temperament tendencies at birth vary somewhat, but when properly raised, an adult Welsh Terrier should be outgoing, energetic, playful, and friendly. Devoted to their owners, individual Welshies show affection in different ways. Some want to be lapdogs, smothering you with kisses; others prefer to lie attentively near you, showing proper gratitude for pats and neck rubs. I've had both types and loved them all.

Blended uniquely with the Welsh Terrier's calm demeanor is a strong prey drive. All dogs possess some degree of prey drive, but it is generally stronger in certain types of dogs, such as terriers, hounds, retrievers, and herding dogs. This means they have a powerful instinct to hunt or chase prey. The dangerous earthwork of this breed's early days required an intense focus and strong will that still exist today. Some people find this mental strength and intensity a problem, but with a little know-how, it can actually be very useful in training a Welsh.

Small animals, running children, moving cars, bikes, and skateboards may all excite your dog's prey drive. While you cannot extinguish it completely, in some situations, you can somewhat desensitize a Welshie to certain things that excite the hunting instinct or redirect the dog's attention.

Welsh Terriers should always be given an acceptable outlet for their prey drive, such as toys or artificial den trials. However, keep in mind that prey drive is not the same thing as aggression toward other dogs or aggression toward people. That's not the correct temperament for a Welshie. If another dog challenges them, this breed won't back down, but a well-bred, properly raised and socialized Welsh Terrier won't instigate aggression with other dogs.

In the early years of the breed, a dog's day was spent patrolling for vermin or hunting in the earth. A Welshie had plenty of space to work out any doggy-politic issues with other canines on the farm. At the end of the day, these hardworking terriers came inside for a well-earned rest. Today's Welsh Terrier doesn't spend the day performing dangerous and exhausting work, and the space it inhabits is limited. Consequently, squabbles between cohabiting dogs can happen when jealousy rears its ugly head.

A Welsh Terrier that is sociable with dogs away from home can be prone to jealousy on its own turf. I have observed some dogs become jealous when another canine in the home gets attention from their

Chapter 1: History and Description

Ch. Rubicon's Sugar Bear, CD, OA, OAJ, NJP, ME, CG, CGC

person. An owner must be a firm, consistent leader to maintain peace in a multiple-dog home with a Welsh Terrier. Welsh Terriers have strong personalities, and if an owner is not willing to be the leader, these dogs will step into the leadership void and take control. A dog that would be a wonderful companion with an owner who is a firm leader can quickly

Photo Courtesy of Jane Latheron

become a little tyrant with a too-lenient owner.

For this and other reasons, Welshies are better suited to a modern home environment where they are the only dog, or there is only one other dog. If there is a second dog in the home, it often works best to have dogs of opposite sexes.

Welsh Terriers will not tolerate physical abuse, torment, or teasing. This could cause them to become aggressive to defend themselves. For this reason, an adult should always supervise young children with a Welsh Terrier, even after the dog is trained. (This is a good rule to follow with all dog breeds.) Welshies should not be left alone to babysit young children. In fact, in a family with kids of any age, all of them need to be taught how to interact with their Welsh Terrier, and the dog also needs to learn how to behave with humans of all ages. A Welshie can be an affectionate companion for children, but only with proper vigilance and training of both the kids and the canine.

Welsh Terriers are watchful and alert to all their senses, which means they can be easily distracted. They are also very sensible, extremely intelligent, and easy to train by someone who knows how to focus their attention. The modern training methods of positive reinforcement work well with this breed. Woe to the owner who underestimates the intelligence of a Welsh Terrier because a Welshie is always learning, even when you don't intend to teach.

One of my Welsh Terriers once watched attentively as I cut hundreds of daffodils to be used as part of the décor at a friend's wedding. An entire year later, this same dog watched again as I was cutting a few daffodils. Then, he suddenly started running and grabbing daffodil flowers, ripping them from their stalks. I was so stunned, and it happened so quickly that I didn't even try to stop him. A moment later, my Welshie ran to me with the last flower hanging from his mouth and wagging his tail. I thanked him for the flower as I took it from his mouth, and I never again cut flowers while he was watching.

Welsh Terriers really want to work for their owners and will sometimes figure out their own jobs. They can be very creative when inventing one. They are "people" dogs that should live in the home rather than outdoors. They crave the company of humans and aren't happy left outside for hours without human attention. A Welshie may bark because it wants to come into the house. However, this breed is not typically yappy. When a Welsh barks, it is barking for a reason. Perhaps, for example, it has been left in a yard where it can see squirrels running around. Barking is part of the breed's natural hunting instinct. It is up to owners not to put their terrier in this situation for lengthy periods and expect the dogs to stay quiet.

Some people mistakenly believe that allowing a Welsh Terrier to participate in artificial den trials teaches the dogs to bark. But Welshies already know how to bark, and they already possess a prey drive. An artificial den trial simply gives a dog an approved outlet for such an impulse. It is the owner's responsibility to acclimate a dog to normal occurrences and to keep it from barking, say, when someone knocks on the front door. My Welshies have always been very quiet in the house once they've understood life's normal occurrences.

Even though Welsh Terriers were originally bred to hunt and dig in the earth, I've found that they are not random diggers. When they dig, it is with a purpose. If a yard has moles or voles or some other vermin burrowing underground, a Welshie is likely to dig to the creature. Welshies may also try to dig under a fence if they desperately want to get out or get to something on the other side. So, it is best not to leave them alone in a yard for long periods of time. The earth beneath fences for Welsh Terriers should have reinforcements to prevent dogs from digging out.

It's important to keep in mind that the Welsh Terrier is a rugged breed originally created for a very dangerous job. They do not suffer fools or tolerate abuse. These are intense and intelligent "people" dogs with a lot of prey drive and a strong will. In the right home (with or without children), a Welshie makes an incredibly attentive and playful companion that is happy to accompany its family on life's adventures.

Is a Welsh Terrier a Good Fit for You?

How do you know if a Welsh Terrier is right for you and your family? To determine this, you first need to carefully evaluate yourself and your circumstances. Next, you need to research the breed.

This book is a good beginning for breed research, and you will find additional resources listed at the end of it. You can also contact reputable breeders to get their input and visit dog events to observe Welsh Terriers and talk with Welsh fanciers in person. You should do all of this before you decide whether this is the breed for you. Once you have gathered as much information as possible, you can compare the breed characteristics with your needs and circumstances to decide if this would be a suitable match.

A Welsh Terrier can be a silly, playful, attentive, intelligent, and devoted pet in the right home, but it is also a strong-willed, intense, and energetic dog with a high prey drive. As touched on earlier, this breed requires an owner who is a leader, teacher, cheerleader, exercise buddy, and companion to his or her dog. It also helps if the owner has a sense of humor. If you lead with patience, firmness, and consistency and reward good behavior, a Welshie will follow you wholeheartedly.

Welsh Terriers are very adaptable to their environment, so while a home with a fenced yard is ideal for them, they can do well as apartment dogs if provided with enough exercise. Any area where a Welsh will be loose should be fenced for the dog's protection and to avoid troublesome encounters with other animals.

Welsh Terriers have a lot of energy, but they are not self-exercisers, so you will need to exercise them regularly. If you put them in a fenced yard alone, they won't jog or run around the yard mindlessly. An intense session of fetch or a 15- to-30-minute brisk walk twice a day will provide the minimum amount of physical exertion needed for an adult Welshie. Teenage dogs will need more exercise. Puppies need more frequent but shorter and less strenuous periods of exercise every day, and they should not be left alone for long periods of time.

Welsh Terriers also need mental stimulation so they don't become bored and get into mischief. Here are a few ways to provide mental stimulation for a Welshie:

- Trick training
- A puzzle toy
- A treat-dispensing ball that makes a dog work for treats
- A chew toy stuffed with peanut butter.

Although these dogs have a high prey drive, it's possible for them to be introduced at a young age to cats and other small animals in a household. An owner must teach a young Welshie how to live with other animals and must remain ever vigilant. If you have small children and aren't capable of always supervising them with a dog, don't get a Welsh Terrier. If you do get one, you'll need to have the time to teach your dog how to behave with your children and to teach your children how to treat a dog.

If you don't want to be a leader and prefer to let your dog do what it wants, don't get a Welsh Terrier. No dog of any breed is born knowing how to be a good pet, but some dogs require less training than a Welsh Terrier. There are breeds with a more submissive nature, a lower prey drive, lower energy, and less need for human companionship. Don't get a Welsh Terrier just because you like its looks and think you can change its characteristic temperament and behavior. That rarely works out well. Get a dog whose temperament, behavior, and lifestyle needs fit yours. If that happens to be a Welsh Terrier, you won't regret it.

CHAPTER 2

Life Stages of the Welsh Terrier

The Puppy

Whatever the age of your Welsh Terrier, it's interesting to know how dogs develop. All canines go through several distinct developmental stages as puppies.

Welsh Terriers are born without sight or hearing. They respond to touch and smell, are totally reliant on their dam (mother), and need food, warmth, and sleep. They also need stimulation from their dam to pee and poop. Responsible breeders begin handling their puppies several times a day as soon as they are born. Nail clipping should start in the first week.

Puppies' eyes open at around two weeks, and their hearing develops soon after. Now, they interact with their littermates and their dam. A breeder will continue to handle puppies and speak to them in soft tones. Toys should be provided, but initially, a puppy will prefer to play with the other puppies and their dam.

FUN FACT
Breed Popularity

As of 2023, Welsh Terriers were ranked the 109th most popular breed registered with the AKC out of 284 dog breeds. The Welshie's popularity ranking has remained relatively stable since the AKC first recognized the breed in 1888.

Puppies are walking at four weeks of age and beginning to bark. They can also pee and poop without maternal stimulation. This is the time to enrich their environment. (I gave my litters a wobble board, rubber

Chapter 2: Life Stages of the Welsh Terrier

Photo Courtesy of Emily Torson

mats, different types of carpet to play on, and short PVC pipes to crawl through.) When the pups are steady on their feet, the litter can go into the breeder's yard with their dam for short periods of time in good weather.

This is also when their sharp puppy teeth begin to emerge, and they get their first lessons in bite inhibition and impulse control from their dam and their littermates. Those baby teeth are sharp, and puppies like to test them on everything. My husband didn't pay attention when I told him to watch out for our first litter's baby teeth. He held a puppy up to his face and got nipped on the nose by a little male that meant no harm.

Usually weaned by five weeks of age, puppies should continue to interact with their dam if she is willing. This bitch is her puppies' first important instructor and gives discipline as necessary. She teaches her puppies how to behave in the pack. The time spent playing with littermates also provides a puppy with behavioral lessons.

From five to seven weeks, puppies are curious about the world and not very fearful. This is a good time to introduce them to more environmental stimuli. They can get comfortable with a collar and leash, a variety of grooming tools, and spending time alone. Puppies can socialize with a few more adults and children, too. Unless you breed dogs, you probably won't be caring for puppies up to this age. It takes a lot of time, effort, and thought to properly raise puppies through this stage.

Many people get their new puppy at around eight to ten weeks old. This is also approximately the time (eight to ten weeks of age) when puppies go through their first major fear period. It is a normal stage of development. Puppies may be wary and sensitive to their environment during the fear period.

Photo Courtesy of Lloyd Kaniger

Socialization needs to continue, but it is important during the fear period to ensure a puppy's experiences are positive. If something frightens a young Welshie, an owner needs to remain calm. By keeping one's body relaxed, moving unhurriedly, and speaking in a normal and happy tone, a person can show a puppy that there is nothing to worry about. Any curiosity displayed or step taken by a puppy toward a feared object should be rewarded.

Treats and praise for obeying simple commands and toys may help distract a pup from its emotional reaction. Look for positive behavior to reward rather than rewarding the dog's fear. If a situation continues to frighten a young

Welshie, sometimes it's best to calmly remove the dog from that environment. Never try to force a puppy to be brave because that could just make it more fearful.

At eight weeks, a Welsh terrier is too young to be fully house-trained. Puppies need frequent potty breaks but can be encouraged to go potty outside. They won't be physically mature enough to be completely house-trained until they are about six months old, and the occasional accident may occur until they are a year old.

Photo Courtesy of Cindy Arnold

This is a good time to enroll a youngster in puppy kindergarten. (A Welsh Terrier puppy should have received its first set of vaccinations at least seven days before starting any class.) Puppy classes provide good socialization and some very basic lessons for both dog and owner. While too young for formal training at this stage, the Welshie can learn through play training. Food and toys can lure it into desired behavior, which is then rewarded and praised.

Since a puppy's attention span is short, training at home can be divided into brief sessions of several minutes spread throughout the day. Teaching a puppy how to learn is important for developing new pathways in the brain. These pathways will make it easier for a dog to learn things in the future.

From 8 to 12 weeks, puppies are a lot of work. Besides many potty breaks, they need to be fed three or more times a day. They also require socialization and frequent (but brief) periods of play and exercise. An owner must not be too permissive or too strict with a puppy, as this sets the tone for the future relationship with the dog.

A Welsh terrier puppy will start to get permanent teeth at around three months old. This means lots and lots of chewing. They need plenty of proper teething toys and can get mouthy with people. Adult teeth may continue to erupt until a puppy is six to eight months, but intense chewing sometimes continues even after a Welshie has all 42 permanent teeth. Chewing helps the adult teeth set. A dog also chews to explore its environment, relieve stress, clean teeth, and exercise the jaw.

Puppies will become less fearful and more curious about the world at around 12 weeks. It's important to continue socialization, play training, and puppy kindergarten.

At 16 weeks old, a Welshie can still benefit from puppy classes. Providing the youngster with rich and varied experiences and gentle, positive lessons helps it develop into a well-adjusted adult and increases its ability to learn. Positive reinforcement works best for training a Welsh Terrier. Training methods should never involve pain or force.

The Adolescent

Just like humans, dogs go through the terrible teens. Welsh Terriers enter this phase around the age of five or six months. A dog doesn't turn into a horrible adolescent overnight. Instead, behavior changes gradually. It is not just about hormones. Both intact dogs and spayed/neutered dogs go through this stage. The adolescent terrier's brain is changing,

Photo Courtesy of Karen Yeomans

and its body is continuing to grow and mature even though it looks more adult. The timing and length of this stage will vary for individual canines.

Adolescent dogs chew a lot to help their adult teeth set and to explore their environment. They also test boundaries, ignore commands, appear to forget previous lessons and become more independent and impulsive. These adolescents have excessive energy too. Dogs of all types wind up in shelters at this stage because their owners weren't prepared to deal with a teenager.

> **FAMOUS WELSH TERRIERS**
> **Royal Welshie**
>
> Edward VIII, later known as the Duke of Windsor and briefly king of the United Kingdom in 1936, owned a little Welsh Terrier named Gwen when he was a boy. Several photos of the royal Welsh Terrier and the prince survive, and we can only speculate on the bond these two shared.

It's important to continue training and socializing the adolescent Welsh Terrier. As their teenage brains develop, dogs may forget things that were previously learned. If that happens, an owner can take a step back and reteach lessons. Adolescent Welshies may also forget their manners, so they need close supervision with children and other dogs. They need more physical and mental exercise than ever, too. When no one is around to supervise, the adolescent canine should be restricted to a small area where it can't get into trouble.

Sometime between the age of six to eight months, a Welsh terrier will experience a second fear period. This is a natural phase in canine development, and dogs outgrow it in a couple of weeks. Just like the previous fear period, it's important to make sure a Welshie has pleasant experiences during this stage. When something frightens a dog, the handler should maintain a relaxed posture and calm demeanor, speak in a happy tone, and move at a normal, unrushed pace. The calmness of the handler will be reassuring to the dog.

Never praise a dog for being afraid; instead, watch for or lure it into some positive behavior that you can then praise. Any sign of curiosity or steps taken by a Welsh Terrier toward a feared object or situation should be encouraged. A frightened terrier can also be praised and treated for looking at its handler. (Dogs look to their leader for cues on how to react.)

To divert a Welshie's attention from its fear reaction, the dog can be rewarded for obeying simple commands or playing with a toy when something fearful is nearby. (I always carried toys and treats in my pockets for puppies and young dogs. Tug toys were especially good at diverting attention.) Sometimes, though, it may be best to remove the dog from a frightening situation. We should not force a fearful canine to be brave. That could imprint the fear more deeply.

Welsh terriers usually reach their adult height and weight by the age of 11 to 12 months. Now they can transition from puppy food to adult dog food. It takes a little longer for Welshies to reach mental maturity and leave the adolescent phase behind. But this stage will pass, so owners shouldn't despair. With patience, understanding, and proper management, an adolescent Welsh Terrier will blossom into a well-behaved and devoted adult.

The Adult

Welsh Terriers usually reach mental maturity by the age of 17 or 18 months. It happens so gradually that you may not notice. Then one day, you suddenly realize your dog has become calmer, less distractible, less destructive, and more obedient. Your Welshie is now both physically and mentally mature. It no longer requires the strict supervision of its adolescence.

The happy, confidant, and biddable adult Welsh Terrier that now stands before you is the reward for properly raising first the puppy and then the adolescent terrier. If a Welsh Terrier is not educated and socialized as a youngster, it can still learn as an adult. With patience, repetition, and consistency, many necessary behavioral skills and lessons can be taught to an adult dog. It just takes more time and effort than it would have when the dog was younger and its mind more of a blank slate.

The grown-up Welsh Terrier is still a high-energy dog. Providing this adult with both physical and mental stimulation prevents mischief-making boredom, provides pleasure, and can help build a stronger bond between dog and owner. In the physical prime of its life, a Welshie craves the attention and company of its owners.

Photo Courtesy of Steve Ambrosio

This is a great time to pursue new experiences with a Welsh Terrier. They love sharing adventures with their owners, and the time spent together often strengthens the dog-owner bond.

The Senior

Individual dogs age at different rates, even within a breed, but we can estimate when our Welsh Terriers become seniors by using their average life span. Since the average for this breed is 12 to 15 years, we can consider them seniors somewhere between 9 and 11. By that age, the average Welshie has lived three-quarters of its life and entered the last quarter.

That doesn't mean your Welsh Terrier won't live longer than 12 to 15 years. (I have had a number of Welshies that outlived that average.) What this means is that we should watch for the changing needs of an aging dog.

Photo Courtesy of Marc Scholtyssek

A Welsh Terrier may still be very active at 11. I didn't compete in obedience with my dog Bear until he was 11 years old. Six months later, he started competing and earning titles in agility. Bear put the lie to the adage that old dogs can't learn new tricks because he loved to learn new things, even in his old age. When he showed signs of aging, I gradually eased up on his activities.

Physical exertion can help senior dogs maintain quality of life. Exercise keeps muscles strong, helps maintain a proper weight, and may improve heart and brain function. Of course, we should tailor any senior exercise program to the individual Welshie. I let my senior dogs guide me in their exercise tolerance.

Veterinary checkups are also important for an older Welsh Terrier. Health screenings and tests can identify issues early and offer the best chance for successful treatment. Old dogs don't recover as quickly from health problems as young dogs.

At this stage, a Welshie's weight needs close monitoring too. Excess weight is hard on old joints, and weight loss can signal a health problem. Veterinarians can advise on senior diets and supplements. Experienced Welsh Terrier breeders are also an excellent source of information for maintaining a senior dog's quality of life.

Since individual dogs age at different rates, an owner must improvise during a Welsh Terrier's senior years. It is important to watch for any changes so you can make necessary adjustments to an older Welshie's life. It may need to go potty more often, or it may become incontinent, sleep more, move more slowly, or have trouble with stairs. Senior dogs usually require more care and supervision from their owners than they did as adults in their prime.

The canine life span is shorter than the human life span, so we usually outlive our dogs. The goal during a Welshie's senior years is to keep the dog comfortable and enjoying life as much as possible.

CHAPTER 3

Choosing a Welsh Terrier

Buying vs. Adopting

Once you decide to get a Welsh Terrier, you still have a lot of decisions to make. First, think about whether you want to buy from a breeder or adopt from a shelter or rescue group. The initial cost of adoption should be less expensive than buying from a breeder. Just remember that it is not inexpensive to provide a dog with proper care once you own it.

Dogs in shelters or available from a rescue may come with health or behavioral issues, but that is not always the case. Some dogs end up in need of a new home because their owner died or because, due to changed circumstances, someone could no longer keep their dog. With work and patience, a rescue Welsh Terrier with behavioral problems may turn into your dream dog. Dogs with health issues may still provide love and companionship in the right home.

You can compete in American Kennel Club (AKC) events such as agility or obedience with both an unregistered, adopted Welsh Terrier and an AKC-registered dog from a breeder. The AKC Purebred Alternative Listing program allows enrolled purebred dogs of AKC-registerable breeds to compete in their companion and performance events. The conformation ring is the one place where an AKC registration is required to compete.

Whichever route you decide to go, don't be surprised if you wind up on a waiting list. There are not large numbers of Welsh Terriers being bred, and the number of Welshies up for adoption through reputable

Chapter 3: Choosing a Welsh Terrier

Photo Courtesy of Mary Duafala

shelters and breed rescues also tends to be small. If you want a puppy, you may have to buy from a breeder because puppies are rarely available from legitimate shelters or rescue groups.

Age and Sex Considerations

I have raised Welsh Terriers from puppies, and I have acquired some as adults. No matter what age they came into my life, the dogs always bonded closely with me and became wonderful companions. The difference between getting a puppy and getting an adult is primarily the time and effort required.

Taking care of a puppy is much more time-consuming than an adult. Puppies need frequent potty time, playtime, and exercise time. They also require a lot of socializing and training. Puppies should not be left on their own for long periods of time if you want them to grow into well-adjusted adults.

DID YOU KNOW?
Defining Characteristics

Welsh Terriers bear a remarkable resemblance to Airedale Terriers. Both of these long-legged terriers have distinctive black and tan wiry coats and are often given similar haircuts, with beards and long hair on their legs. The easiest way to tell these terriers apart is by their size. Airedale Terriers are the largest terriers, and the males often grow to 23 inches tall and weigh 50 to 70 pounds. In contrast, male Welsh Terriers can reach around 15 inches in height and only weigh about 20 pounds. The Airedale Terrier is believed to have been developed in the 1800s by crossing existing terrier breeds with the Otterhound. Both Welsh and Airedale Terriers are thought to share a common ancestor: an early type of rough-coated black and tan terrier.

Adolescent Welsh Terriers also require a lot of time. They need training, socialization, and plenty of mental and physical exercise. Supervision is also a necessity for adolescents to keep them out of trouble.

If you don't have the time to spend raising a puppy or an adolescent dog, an adult Welsh Terrier may be a good choice. Sometimes, breeders will have an adult available, and these dogs are usually well-socialized and trained. Adults adopted through rescue may have some issues, but a reputable rescue group or shelter will inform potential adopters of any problems and offer guidance.

Even though they don't require as much time, adult Welsh Terriers still need attention from their owners. These are not dogs that will be happy only getting to walk or play with their human family on weekends. They will need some of your attention every day. The more attention you give your Welsh Terrier, the happier it will be.

Senior Welsh Terriers can provide devoted companionship to new owners, and they do it without the high energy and problems associated with youth. Welshies are very adaptable dogs, and senior dogs can and do bond with new people when rehomed.

I have seen no major personality differences between male and female Welsh Terriers. While males tend to be a little larger than the females, the personalities of the dogs are a very individual thing. I have had very sweet and cuddly males and females, and I have had a few of both sexes that disdained sitting in my lap for cuddles but loved "helping" me with any activity. All my Welshies of both sexes always had plenty of prey drive and loved Earthdog activities.

Finding a Responsible Breeder

> *The Welsh Terrier Club of America is the first stop for anyone interested in a Welsh Terrier. The website includes a breeder directory, and all breeders listed are members of the parent club in good standing. Look for breeders who conduct genetic testing—in the case of Welsh Terriers, testing for primary lens luxation is an absolute must. I also recommend looking for breeders who are invested in their dogs and in the preservation of the breed—this means breeders who participate in shows or performance events. Finally, look for breeders who want to know you and know where their puppies are going. Puppies should be a passion, not a product.*
>
> **EMILY CARROLL**
> *Bayleigh Carroway Welsh Terriers*

A responsible Welsh Terrier breeder specializes in the breed and has a wealth of knowledge about the breed and the individual dogs' pedigrees. They often breed only Welsh Terriers but may breed one or two other breeds. These breeders sell their puppies directly to pet owners without a middleman. They do not sell their puppies in pet stores.

Properly caring for a litter of puppies is a lot of work, so most reputable breeders will have only one or two litters at a time. They won't have a constant supply of puppies but may keep a waiting list of people who want a puppy.

Good breeders only breed healthy dogs with excellent temperaments that are proper examples of the breed. They do health screenings and genetic testing on dogs before breeding. This doesn't guarantee that their

Photo Courtesy of Stephen Long

puppies never have any health issues, but they are more likely to produce healthy dogs with good temperaments. Such breeders raise puppies in a safe and loving environment and give them the best possible start in life. Also, if a Welsh Terrier purchased from a reputable breeder ever has a problem, expert advice is only a phone call away.

Look for a breeder who registers dogs with the primary national registry in your country. In the United States, that is the AKC. The primary registry in Canada is the Canadian Kennel Club (CKC); be careful not to confuse it with the Continental Kennel Club (CKC).

Unfortunately, registration papers don't guarantee the health and temperament of a puppy, and they don't guarantee a dog comes from a reputable breeder. The first place to look for a responsible Welsh Terrier breeder is the national breed club. In the United States, that is the Welsh Terrier Club of America (WTCA). This organization is devoted to preserving the breed and promoting responsible breeding and ownership of Welsh Terriers. One of the organization's goals is to educate and offer guidance to prospective owners.

Very often, but not always, responsible breeders will be members of their national breed club. You can contact the WTCA for a list of member breeders. There are also regional Welsh Terrier clubs that can put you in touch with responsible breeders in their region. The WTCA should be able to tell you if there is a regional club in your area.

You can narrow down a list of Welsh Terrier breeders in the United States by choosing those who take part in AKC events (particularly conformation shows) with their dogs. Good breeders want the temperament, structure, and movement of their dogs judged against the breed standard by knowledgeable experts in the show ring. It helps them see what they have gotten right in their breeding program and what they need to improve. It also allows them to see what other breeders' dogs they want to include in their breeding program.

They may also take part in Earthdog, agility, obedience, and other activities. I believe participation in canine performance events helps educate breeders about aspects of the breed they may not experience in the conformation ring. On the other hand, some of the top professional dog show handlers specializing in terriers are among the most knowledgeable dog people I have met. They must understand the dogs inside and out to win the top prizes with the canines they show.

The AKC is another good source of information for people looking for purebred dogs. On their website, you can find information for national breed clubs, regional clubs, and local kennel clubs around the country as well as advice for dog owners. Local kennel clubs can also be helpful. They may know of Welsh breeders in their area. They may also provide information about area dog shows that usually have a large terrier entry.

Attending dog shows is a good way to meet terrier fanciers in your area. If no Welshies are entered, exhibitors showing other terrier breeds often know people involved with the Welsh. If the breed is being shown, you can observe and possibly meet the dogs and their people afterward. (Don't approach people when they are about to enter the ring with their dogs, in the ring, or rushing between classes.)

Responsible Welsh Terrier breeders usually belong to at least one AKC-registered club: the national breed club, a regional club, or a local kennel club. They also take advantage of educational opportunities to stay abreast of canine health issues, new training techniques, etc. Ask breeders what clubs they belong to.

Photo Courtesy of Vic Keisker

You don't want to buy from a puppy mill or irresponsible breeder whose only concern is profit rather than the welfare of the dogs. Anyone can create a fancy website or advertisement, but you must look beneath the glitz to make sure the dogs are healthy, well-kept, properly raised, and good representatives of the breed.

Irresponsible breeders rarely screen their dogs for health issues or perform genetic tests before breeding. Quick profit is the primary concern of these breeders, not the health, temperament, or even the breed standard. Their puppies may be raised in poor conditions, which may traumatize the dogs and lead to behavioral issues. These puppies may also be unhealthy because of their unfortunate start in life or an unhealthy parent.

Buying from irresponsible breeders perpetuates a business that is horrendous for the dogs involved. Don't help them stay in business by buying one of their puppies. If you have worries about a specific breeder in the United States, you can reach out to the WTCARES chairperson and ask if the rescue has concerns regarding that breeder. Sad to say, this nonprofit rescue for Welsh Terriers has a lot of experience with dogs bred and sold by irresponsible breeders. WTCARES may not give you specifics, but if the rescue says they have a lot of experience with a particular breeder, take that as a warning sign.

Communicating with Your Breeder

Many responsible breeders are not independently wealthy and have full-time jobs, so the first thing to remember when calling a breeder is to call at a reasonable time for their time zone. If you email them, you

Chapter 3: Choosing a Welsh Terrier

may not get a response for a few days. Give them a little time to respond. Unfortunately, there are always a few breeders who won't respond unless they have puppies available. Don't let a nonresponse stop your search; just move on to other breeders.

When you first speak to a breeder about finding a Welsh Terrier, they should ask you questions about yourself, your lifestyle, and your situation. They should also ask for references and may want to visit your home. If they don't ask questions and request either references or a visit to your home before agreeing to sell you a dog, that should be a red flag. If someone immediately offers to sell you a puppy, don't buy a dog from them. The interview process between a breeder and puppy buyer should comprise more than one brief phone call, email exchange, or meeting.

The most important thing to do when a breeder asks questions is to answer honestly. Even if you think your answer won't please a breeder, it is better to tell the truth rather than what you think they want to hear. Responsible breeders ask questions to determine if you will be a good fit for a Welsh Terrier, and they need honest answers. Just because you want a Welsh Terrier doesn't mean that you will be happy living with one or that a Welshie would be happy in your home. Please trust the breeder to figure out if you're a good match for a Welsh Terrier.

You may hear a breeder refer to some puppies as show puppies and others as pet puppies. Don't be put off by these labels. The most important job of any Welsh Terrier is to be a good pet. Show dogs may be good enough to be bred in the future, but even they will be someone's pet. Responsible breeders are just as devoted to their pet puppies as they are to show puppies.

When a breeder is finished asking you questions, ask them if this breed is a good fit for you and your lifestyle. If they say you are not a good fit for the breed, think carefully before continuing your search for a Welsh Terrier. If the dog-owner match isn't good, you and your family and the dog will all end up unhappy.

One of the most important questions to ask a breeder is whether you can meet the puppies and see where they have been raised. If they don't allow people to visit, then you should look for another breeder.

Even during a pandemic, outdoor visits with people wearing masks should be okay. You may not be able to see indoors where the dogs are kept and raised, but you can make some judgments based on the conditions you see and your interaction with the puppies outdoors. Responsible breeders keep their dogs in a clean, spacious, uncrowded environment.

You should be able to meet the dam (mother) of a litter. If the dam is not on the breeder's property because she lives in a pet home when not raising puppies, ask the breeder to arrange for you to meet the dam. Besides passing on her DNA, the dam raises the puppies for the first weeks of their lives, so she is an important influence. Sometimes you can also meet the sire (father), but the sire will not necessarily live with or belong to the breeder.

Here are some additional questions to ask the breeder about themselves and their operation:

1. How many litters do you breed each year?
2. Do you require a contract? Is there a health guarantee? Is there a spay/neuter clause? Or do you spay/neuter your puppies before they go to their new homes?
3. At what age do you let buyers take their puppies? A responsible breeder never places puppies before they are eight weeks old. Many breeders wait until puppies are even older than eight weeks before placing them. This gives them more time to prepare the dogs for their future life.
4. What support can I expect if I purchase a Welsh Terrier from you?
5. Can you put me in contact with some of your previous puppy buyers? If the answer is no, ask why. Unless this is their first litter, a responsible breeder should be happy to provide former puppy buyers as references.
6. Will you take the dog back if I cannot keep it in the future? Responsible breeders usually stipulate in their contract that they be contacted if you can no longer keep the dog and will take responsibility for it.
7. What do you think of WTCARES? Responsible breeders in the United States are supportive of the work WTCARES does. They will never ask you not to contact the rescue.

Questions to ask a breeder about their puppies:

- What type of registration will my dog have, regular or limited? The AKC offers a Limited Registration for individual dogs that provides the individual dog with registration, but no puppies it produces will be eligible for registration. A dog with an AKC Limited Registration can still compete and earn titles in AKC performance and companion events. It is meant as a protection for the puppy, and a breeder has the option to change this registration to a regular AKC registration in the future.
- Tell me about the parents of this litter. What are their temperaments like? What titles do they have?
- How often are your puppies handled each day? How many people have they interacted with? (Or how many will they interact with before placement?) What about interactions with children?
- Do you start house-training your puppies before they are sold?
- Are your puppies crate trained? A crate is not an instrument of torture, and it can be a very useful tool. Dogs that are properly crate trained will consider it a safe place. It is also a secure place for dogs to ride in the car.
- Are your puppies used to wearing a collar?

Health Tests and Certifications and Questions

Welsh Terriers are a healthy breed, but health problems that also affect many other breeds sometimes affect them. According to the website for Bow Wow Meow Pet Insurance in Australia, Welshies have only an average chance of developing health issues during their life, so they are more affordable to insure than some other breeds. (We'll take a brief look at pet health insurance in Chapter 8.)

Some health problems that can occur in Welsh Terriers are primary lens luxation/glaucoma, cataracts, allergies, epilepsy, hypothyroidism, hip dysplasia, Legge-Calve-Perthes, and congenital megaesophagus.

There is a genetic test that allows breeders to screen for primary lens luxation (PLL) prior to breeding. This is a serious condition that is

Photo Courtesy of Krystle Sickman

painful for the dog and can lead to blindness. The WTCA recommends breeders use the PLL DNA test. Puppy buyers should ask about the PLL status of the sire and dam and check the authenticity of test results on the Orthopedic Foundation for Animals (OFA) website.

There are three possible results with the PLL DNA test: affected, carrier, or clear. Dogs have two copies of the gene tested for PLL and inherit one from each parent. An affected/high-risk dog has two copies of the mutated gene that causes PLL and is at high risk of developing it. If bred, an affected dog will pass on one copy of the mutated gene that causes PLL. A dog that is a carrier has one normal gene and one copy of the mutated gene that causes PLL. It has only a slight risk of ever developing PLL (the reason is not yet understood), and if bred, it has a 50% chance of passing on a clear copy of the gene rather than the mutation. Dogs that test clear do not have the genetic mutation known to cause PLL in Welsh Terriers and can only pass on the normal/clear gene to any offspring.

Don't be alarmed if a breeder has bred a PLL-clear Welsh Terrier to a PLL carrier. The gene pool for Welsh Terriers is small, and removing otherwise healthy dogs that are PLL carriers would further shrink the gene pool and possibly create other health problems in the breed. If carriers are only bred to dogs that are PLL clear, the risk for this disease is diminished and can be eliminated from the breed gradually without further shrinking the gene pool for Welsh Terriers.

There is also one genetic test some breeders are using, but that is not, at this time, recommended for the breed by the OFA. That is the degenerative myelopathy (DM) DNA test. This disease affects older dogs in some breeds, causing a degeneration of the spinal cord and gradual paralysis. Even though some Welsh Terriers test as At Risk or Carriers with the DM DNA test, no one knows what role this gene mutation plays in Welsh Terriers or if the dogs ever develop the disease. The University of Missouri, which developed the test, has, so far, not histologically verified the occurrence of this disease in the breed. (Check the OFA website for any changes to their breed recommendations concerning the DM DNA test.)

Dog breeding is both a science and an art, and good breeders use medical tools wisely to maintain and improve the health of the breed.

Here are a few health-related questions to ask a breeder:

- Can you provide the name and contact information for your veterinarian?
- Will you provide the puppy's full medical history and vaccine record? Don't buy a puppy from a breeder who is unwilling to produce medical records for their puppies. Don't buy a puppy from a breeder if their puppies have had no vaccinations or have not been dewormed prior to placement. Avoid breeders whose puppies have not been examined by a licensed veterinarian.
- What health testing do you do?
- Can I see the health clearances and test results for the sire and dam? You can verify test results by contacting the veterinarian that performed the test. For OFA tests and health certifications, check the OFA website to find the results for specific dogs.

Tips for Picking Your Puppy

> *Don't choose a dog just because it's cute—they're all cute! Watch them interact with the breeder or foster, as well as with any other dogs in their environment. Look for a healthy dog that is well cared for and clean. Be sure to see the environment that the puppy is raised in and what the personalities of the parents or adult dogs in the household are like. That is who raised your puppy and taught it how to react or respond to situations.*
>
> **ANNE PELLETIER**
> *Bremadog Welsh*

Imagining the adult dog that a puppy will become can be difficult. With all their knowledge and experience, good breeders can help you pick the individual puppy that is best suited to you. They can also help educate you about caring for and training your new pet.

If you are a first-time dog or terrier owner, you probably don't want a puppy that is extremely bossy with the other puppies. That dominant individual could be difficult for an inexperienced owner to train. Likewise, the puppy with unlimited energy that continues to play when the rest of the litter takes a break is probably not going to be the easiest to raise. It is unusual for a Welsh puppy to be shy, but if there is one, I advise against choosing this puppy. It is not the correct temperament for a Welsh.

Typically, a Welsh Terrier puppy that is curious, friendly, outgoing, and confident (but not the most energetic or bossiest member of a litter) will make a good pet. Look for eyes that are bright and clear, a shiny coat, healthy skin, and clean ears. A dog's poop should be firm (not loose or runny) and well-formed with no blood or mucus. Make sure there are no signs of diarrhea stains on the puppy's bottom. Watch for normal movement at all speeds and a good energy level.

Researching Rescues

You need to do some research before adopting to make sure the rescue group that you get a dog from is legitimate. There are irresponsible breeders masquerading as rescue groups because rescuing dogs has become popular. These sham rescues/breeders spend very little on the care and raising of their dogs and profit by charging an adoption fee. Do your research so you don't help these scammers stay in business by adopting from them.

A legitimate rescue will inform you of potential issues with a Welsh Terrier available for adoption. Their primary concern is making sure their dogs wind up in suitable, loving homes, receiving proper care. They will not rush the adoption process. They will work with you to make sure you adopt a dog that is a good fit for your family.

Rescue groups usually foster dogs with very experienced people capable of evaluating them. Daily close contact with a dog allows a foster

Chapter 3: Choosing a Welsh Terrier

Photo Courtesy of Katie Cane

parent to gain valuable information and insights about the animal. Living in foster homes also helps maintain or improve a canine's social abilities. When dealing with a rescue, remember their workers are volunteers and usually have families, jobs, and otherwise busy lives. Treat these unpaid volunteers with respect.

Some rescues are dedicated to helping only one breed, and they have networks of knowledgeable and hardworking volunteers. The ONLY legitimate rescue group specifically for Welsh Terriers in the United States is WTCARES. The mission of this charitable nonprofit is to rescue and rehome Welsh Terriers in need. WTCARES' only concern is the welfare of Welsh Terriers. Their very specialized knowledge and understanding of Welsh Terriers is of significant benefit to dogs and their adopters.

There are also rescue groups dedicated to all dogs and some for all types of terriers, not just Welsh Terriers. If you find a Welsh Terrier with one of these rescues, you can reach out to WTCARES for advice about the legitimacy of the group.

There are a variety of animal shelters operating in the United States. Some well-funded nonprofit shelters have trained staff members to evaluate their dogs. Unfortunately, high-volume municipal shelters with limited funds do not always have the time or enough expert staff to conduct detailed behavioral evaluations of their wards. It may be advisable to take an experienced terrier trainer/owner with you to evaluate a Welsh Terrier in a municipal shelter.

Some of the better-funded shelters will have veterinarians and vet techs on staff to care for the animals. Facilities with very limited budgets may only provide the basics of food and shelter, and their dogs may not have been evaluated for more than basic healthcare issues. No matter what level of medical care a shelter provides, an adopted Welsh Terrier should be taken for a veterinary checkup as soon as possible after adoption.

You will find both kill and no-kill shelters. The term "no-kill" typically means a facility doesn't euthanize healthy, nonaggressive animals. Some well-funded no-kill shelters may keep dogs until they are placed. Other no-kill facilities may need to euthanize canines to make room for more animals when capacity is reached.

There are still some high-volume municipal shelters that euthanize many dogs every year. These tend to be low-budget facilities where dogs stay for a limited time before being put down. Their adoption process is often uncomplicated and inexpensive. You may be able to adopt a dog on the same day you apply. When considering a shelter dog that's just days from euthanasia, try to take an experienced terrier person with you to evaluate it. You'll have little time to decide, and a Welsh Terrier may not be on its best behavior in such a noisy, crowded kennel environment.

The adoption process for every organization and facility is different. While the path from application to approval at some low-budget kill shelters may be quick and easy, rescue groups and better-funded no-kill shelters typically have lengthier processes. Just like a breeder, they will ask many questions about you and your lifestyle. They may require a referral from your veterinarian and even a home inspection. This can seem arduous, but it is to ensure the dog is a good fit for you.

The adoption fee will also vary with each group and facility. Always try to research an organization to make sure your payment will cover the humane care of a dog in a legitimate rescue or shelter rather than fund a puppy mill.

Additional things to look for in a good shelter and rescue group:

- They require a contract.
- They require the return of a dog when a placement doesn't work out.
- They only place dogs that are spayed or neutered. (A shelter with limited funding may require you to have the dog spayed/neutered and sometimes provides a certificate to cover a partial cost of the surgery.)
- They provide proof of vaccination and health records.

Tips for Adopting a Welsh Terrier

- Don't wait until you see a dog you like on the WTCARES website to put in an adoption application. It takes time for them to evaluate an applicant.
- Ask about the dog's history, if it knows any basic commands, if it has any known behavioral issues, and whether it is house-trained. (If a shelter does not have a lot of information on a dog, take a trainer or experienced terrier person to meet the dog before deciding to adopt.)
- Consider whether you have time for a Welshie that is not house-trained or has behavioral issues. Have a plan to deal with any issues before adopting a dog.
- Ask if the dog has any medical issues and, if so, consider whether you have the time and money for the special care it will require. Speak to a veterinarian about the medical issues before adopting.

CHAPTER 4

Preparing for Your Welsh Terrier

Like an expectant parent, you need to prepare for the arrival of your Welsh Terrier. Everyone in the household should be involved. Before the dog arrives, there should be a household meeting to discuss responsibilities for its care. Decide who will feed, exercise, train, and take the terrier outside regularly, and develop a timetable. Playtime needs to be included in the schedule too. All canines, both puppies and adults, thrive on routine.

Photo Courtesy of Linda Brisbin

You should also discuss when your new Welshie will arrive. It's best if all household members are home and can spend time with your new terrier during the dog's first few days with you. For a busy working family, that may mean a long weekend.

Everyone will need to follow the same rules with the dog. Otherwise, it will be confused. Discuss the household regimen and rules for your terrier:

- Is your Welshie allowed on the furniture?
- Where will the dog sleep?
- Where will the dog eat?
- Are some areas off-limits to your pet?
- How will you handle the mistakes your dog makes?

Everyone should agree on your Welshie's call name and on some common words and phrases to use with it. For instance, will you ask your dog if it wants to "go out" or "go for a walk?" Will you tell your terrier to go "to bed" or "to your place?" Things will be less confusing for your new dog if everyone uses the same terminology.

If a Welsh Terrier already knows certain words, you'll want to use those, but you may not have that information. When Bear first came to live with me, he didn't seem to understand the command "down." I discovered he was trained to lie down on the command of "drop," and that word worked like a charm. It's easier to use commands the dog already knows, but a Welshie can adjust if you do things differently. Just be sure everyone in the household is using the same words with your terrier.

Getting Your Children and Current Pets Ready

If you have children who are not used to dogs, you'll want to teach them how to behave with one before you bring yours home. Ask a friend with a child-friendly dog to help teach your children how to approach and pet it.

Young children need to understand that canines dislike hugs and kisses; they prefer to be petted. Children also need to know that your terrier needs alone time, and when your dog is in its crate or own area, they should not bother it. Make a rule that they must not disturb the animal when it's eating or sleeping. In fact, they should never handle the Welshie unless an adult is supervising.

If you already have a dog at home, you will want to make sure that it is healthy and up-to-date on vaccinations before bringing your new terrier home. This is especially important if you are getting a young Welshie that has not yet received all its puppy shots. Talk to your veterinarian to find out if your current pet needs a checkup before the arrival of your new dog.

Plan where, when, and how you will introduce your pets. You should also pick up all the dog toys and arrange for separate feeding and sleeping areas for each animal. Don't leave them together when you are not at home until they have completely bonded. If your new terrier is a puppy, I suggest keeping the dogs separated when you are not home until the youngster matures.

If you have a cat, create a safe, dog-free room where it can escape your Welshie's attention. The cat's food, toys, and litter box should be placed out of the terrier's reach. You also need to ensure there are high

Photo Courtesy of Veronika Holásková

places, like cat trees or shelves, where the cat can escape the dog in rooms they will share. (We'll look at introducing your Welsh Terrier to your cat in the next chapter. Initially, you'll want to keep the dog and cat in separate rooms where they cannot see each other.)

Other small animals, such as gerbils or hamsters, should be kept well out of the dog's reach.

Preparing Your Home

> *Welshies can be escape artists and often have selective hearing on recall. They are small and fast, so guard all doors when opening them, and leash or crate Welshies when people are going in or out. Baby gates are great when separation is needed, and physically fenced yards are a must for exercise and playtime.*
>
> **ELIZABETH BERRY**
> *Airedale and Welsh Terrier Rescue*

You want to dog-proof your home before getting your new terrier. Canines are like babies. They investigate with their mouth and chew on and swallow things they shouldn't. Try to look at your house from the animal's point of view. Sometimes it helps to get down on your hands and knees so you can better see things from their perspective.

Move things like medicines, chemicals, cleaners, mousetraps, insect bait stations, and poisonous plants out of the dog's reach. Elevate or hide electrical cords and phone and computer wires so your terrier can't chew on them. You can also cover cords and wires with protectors or PVC.

Check the floor, low shelves, and coffee tables for things your pet may chew, swallow, or break. Things like small toys, paper clips, and coins can be dangerous for a dog.

Make sure closets and floor-level cabinets are kept closed and cannot be opened by a Welshie. To be safe, move dangerous items from closet floors and low cabinets to somewhere higher that is impossible for the animal to reach.

Trash cans should be untippable and tall enough the dog won't be able to get into them. The cans should also have secure lids. It is easier to prevent your pet from getting into the trash than to deal with a vet emergency because the dog ate something it shouldn't have.

Tie up any long window blind cords to prevent your terrier from eating the strings or getting tangled and strangled.

A Safe Space for Your Dog

You want to create a small area for your Welshie to stay in when you cannot supervise it. This is to protect the terrier (until it settles in or is mature) and the house. The goal is for your pet to feel it can eat and sleep in this area without being disturbed. (If you have children, it's very important for your Welsh Terrier to have an area where they are not allowed to bother him. That needs to be a rule.)

The floor in this space should be easy to clean, and it should not be too isolated. You want your dog to be able to see some household activity but also to be safe from disturbances. A suitable location is usually the kitchen, and if it is too large, you can temporarily gate off a section or set up a small exercise pen. Your Welshie's crate or bed can be placed in this spot. (Leave the crate door open so the dog can go in and out as it pleases during the day.)

Preparing Outside Spaces

You also need to prepare any outdoor spaces your dog may be using.

If you have a fenced-in yard, the ideal physical fence for an energetic and athletic Welsh Terrier is six feet high. Even though this breed is not that tall, they can jump quite high and only need to hook their front feet on the top of the fence to pull up and over.

I realize local regulations may not always allow a six-foot fence. It is possible to modify a slightly shorter fence (no lower than four and a half feet) to discourage a Welsh from jumping or climbing out of the yard. You can add a section of fencing that tilts inward. Coyote Rollers on top of a fence can be an effective solution too. Planting shrubs in front of the fence to limit the dog's access may also help.

Welshies are very capable climbers when it suits them, so a solid privacy fence is preferable to a see-through fence such as chain link. The solid-type boundary is not easily climbed and has the bonus effect of restricting your pet's view of enticing attractions beyond it. Solid fencing also limits the chances of a dog inside the yard being teased by someone on the outside.

> **HELPFUL TIP**
> **Prey Drive Precautions**
>
> Welsh Terriers have a profoundly ingrained prey drive, often considered a holdover from their early days as hunting dogs. As a result, Welsh Terriers may not be a good fit for a family with cats or rodents in the home. However, dogs with high prey drive can generally live in homes with small children, provided that the adults take appropriate precautions and do not leave children unattended with the dog. Before bringing your Welsh Terrier home, ensure that your yard has adequate fencing, and always keep your dog on a leash when outside your yard or home—you never know when a squirrel will catch its eye!

Now that we've looked at the top of the fence, we need to consider the bottom. Terriers are bred to burrow into the earth to reach prey, and they can quickly tunnel through soft earth beneath a fence to get out of a yard. You can bury chicken wire under a fence to discourage digging.

Next, walk the fence line and look for any gaps or weak spots your dog might use to escape. Make sure there are no items that could be used as a ladder to get over the fence. Things like lawn chairs, garbage cans, and woodpiles should be moved away.

Check the gate latches to make sure they're secure and won't open if your terrier bumps into the fence. For children or anyone else in the household who doesn't always remember to close gates, you can install one that will automatically close after someone opens it.

There are situations where a physical fence is not an option. In those circumstances, you can consider an invisible one for your yard. It would never be my first choice, but if you are willing to closely monitor your pet, this can work for a Welshie. You must train a canine to respect the

Photo Courtesy of Ellen King

boundaries of invisible fencing, and even then, it offers no protection against other animals or strangers who choose to come into your yard. If extremely excited, a dog could run through the electric shock to get outside the fence and later not want to cross back into the yard. I know several Welsh Terrier owners who use invisible fencing, and they all say for it to work, you must monitor your pets when they're outside.

A fence is not meant to make a dog a prisoner of your yard but rather to keep it in a secure playground. You should also be aware that a Welsh Terrier will not be happy left outside alone for long periods of time. These dogs want to be with their owners. Don't leave a Welshie unsupervised in the yard for hours. In fact, a Welshie should never be outside when no one is at home.

Chapter 4: Preparing for Your Welsh Terrier

I do not recommend keeping any unattended dog outside on a tether or chain. It could become entangled in the restraint and injure itself. A tied-out canine is also at risk from aggressive roaming dogs and wild animals, and any passerby can enter the yard to tease or steal your pet. You should only use tethers for short periods of time when you are with your terrier, like at a picnic in the park.

A Welshie can be happy without a fenced-in yard, provided it gets plenty of on-leash exercise with you. On a long line, your dog can romp and play in a park or field without being loose.

If you have an in-ground pool, it should be fenced off to prevent your pet from falling in accidentally. Make sure the pool gate latches securely and regularly check for fence areas that need to be repaired or reinforced.

Toxic plants should be fenced off or removed from the dog's yard. Some common garden plants, such as Lily-of-the-Valley, are very poisonous. Check the plants in your yard to make sure they will not pose a danger to your Welshie. For toxic bulbs buried at least a few inches in the earth, like daffodils or tulips, you can fasten chicken wire over the soil to prevent a curious puppy from digging. (In my experience, adult Welsh Terriers only dig when bored or there is prey, such as a mole underground, but it is better to be safe with toxic bulbs.)

Curious canines will sometimes chew on garden mulch, so make sure there is *no cocoa bean mulch* in your yard, as it is extremely toxic for dogs. Pine and cedar mulch are safer options, but it's always a good idea to provide your pet with chew toys so mulch isn't such a temptation for munching.

Avoid using toxic chemicals in any area the dog will use, and move garden supplies and tools out of its reach. Just like inside the house, garbage cans must be untippable and have secure lids to keep a Welsh Terrier out.

Talk to local dog owners and veterinarians to find out if there are any specific issues you should know about in your area. There are some outdoor issues that may be regional, such as poisonous reptiles. For example, I know one Welsh Terrier owner whose dogs successfully completed snake-aversion training.

Get the Essentials

Now it's time to make sure you have some essential canine supplies. Gathering these items beforehand will make the transition into your household easier. If you've already owned a dog, you may have what you need. However, it's best to take inventory and stock up before bringing your Welshie home. Once your pet arrives, you want to spend time getting to know each other rather than rushing around shopping.

Some basic items you will need:

1. Food
2. Treats
3. Two non-tip bowls for food and water
4. Crate
   - The crate should be large enough for your Welsh Terrier to stand up, turn around, and sit. If you want to get a crate that will fit a puppy after it grows up, consider one with removable dividers. A cage that is too large is not helpful for potty training. The extra space may disinhibit a dog from soiling in its bed. A crate is useful for travel, potty training, and emergencies. (See Chapter 6 for information on crate training.)
5. Soft, washable bedding for the dog crate
   - For a puppy, it should be chew resistant.
6. Scented articles
   - Ask for an article (such as some bedding or a toy) with the scent of your Welshie's playmates or dam to comfort the dog on its first night with you. If this is a foster dog not living with other dogs, ask for something with the scent of its foster parent. To start introductions ahead of time, you can give your current dog or cat an article scented with their future housemate. Also, consider providing the Welshie with an article scented with his soon-to-be cat or dog roomies. You may need to provide the articles that will be used to carry the scent.
7. Dog bed
   - Even if allowed on the furniture, it's nice for a Welshie to have a bed of its own. Some people have one in every room their terrier hangs out in, but a single bed is usually enough to start with.

8. Collar/ID tag
    - You need a collar on which you can attach your Welsh Terrier's ID tag, rabies tag, and license tag. The ID tag can have your phone number in case your pet gets lost, or you can buy a collar with your phone number stitched into it. If two fingers fit between the dog's neck and collar, it fits correctly. Except for breakaway collars, you should *never leave a collar on a dog* when it's unsupervised, crated, or playing with another dog because there is a danger of strangulation.
9. Collar/harness for walking and exercise
    - Get measurements so you can buy correctly sized equipment. I recommend a martingale (limited-slip) collar for walking and training a young puppy. This type of collar has an extra loop, and if the dog pulls, the collar constricts without choking the dog. The martingale collar prevents a Welsh Terrier puppy, whose head is not much broader than its neck, from slipping or backing out of its collar on a walk. If you prefer to use a harness instead of a collar, research harnesses for your terrier's size before getting one. The harness will need to fit snugly but not too tightly. I am not a fan of head halters. If used improperly, this equipment can snap a canine's head sideways and potentially damage the spine. Some dogs don't like head halters, and certain brands are prone to slipping off.
10. Leash and long line
    - A four-foot leash is a suitable length for a young pup. A six-foot leash works well for older puppies, adolescents, and adults. For safety issues, I recommend a long line of 15 to 20 feet rather than a retractable leash for those times when you are in an unfenced area with your dog. (Never use any kind of long leash near a road. I know of one young terrier that was killed by a car while being walked beside a street on a retractable leash. The puppy saw a squirrel and dashed after it into the path of a car.)
11. Poop bags/pooper scooper
12. Enzyme cleaning products
    - Even if your new dog is already potty trained, accidents can still happen as it adjusts.

13. Pee Pads
    - These are useful when your terrier isn't already house-trained.
14. Baby gates and/or exercise pen
    - These will be helpful for giving your Welshie a safe space of its own to rest and play in when you can't supervise it.
15. Grooming supplies
    - To start, you will want brushes, combs, a nail trimmer, styptic powder, and shampoo. A small grooming table that folds up is not essential, but it is an extremely helpful grooming aid. (We'll take a closer look at grooming a Welsh Terrier in Chapter 7.)
16. Toys
    - You will want a variety of toys to prevent boredom and provide mental and physical stimulation for your terrier. Make sure there are no parts, such as buttons or eyes, that can be chewed off and swallowed. Age-appropriate chew toys, squeaky toys, fetch toys and balls, and food-dispensing toys are all good. Have some toys for outdoors and indoors.

Nutrition

> *Don't over-feed your dog! Every dog has different caloric requirements, depending on their lifestyle. Feel free to adjust the amount you feed as activities change. Use the dog's body as a guide for proper weight—you should be able to feel the ribs under a layer of cushion. If you can't feel the ribs, your dog is too heavy.*
>
> **ANNE PELLETIER**
> *Bremadog Welsh*

The best food to feed your new pet is what it is already eating. You'll want to ask the person from whom you get your Welsh Terrier what it's been eating, so you can stock up ahead of time. (Some breeders give their new owners a small amount of dog food to get them started.) You should keep your Welshie on its old diet for at least a couple of weeks while it settles into your home. Adapting to a new environment is hard enough without also stressing a canine's gastrointestinal system with a different food.

Dogs of all ages should be kept on a regular feeding schedule. This helps them be consistent with their potty times and may provide a sense of stability. It also allows you to closely monitor your pet's appetite. I am not a fan of free feeding. This style of feeding can lead to canine obesity and irregular potty times.

Feed small meals three to four times a day to a Welsh Terrier between the ages of 8 to 12 weeks. From three to six months, feed a puppy three times a day. These multiple small feedings make digestion easier and help growing canines maintain their energy level. Once they reach six months, dogs should transition to just twice-a-day feedings.

Welsh Terriers should eat puppy food from the time they are weaned until around one year old. These foods are specially formulated to meet the demands of their growing body. At one year of age, a Welsh Terrier can transition to adult dog food. It is generally recommended that adults be fed two times per day, though they can manage on just one meal a day.

Older terriers generally do well with twice-a-day feeding. Consider a specially formulated senior food when your Welshie slows down with age. A breeder who has successfully navigated the geriatric years of their own Welsh Terriers can offer valuable advice on feeding your older pet.

Whatever the age of your Welsh Terrier, if you are feeding a commercial dog food, it's usually a good idea to follow the manufacturer's feeding guidelines. Just watch to make sure your Welshie maintains a good body weight. If it seems to lose weight or get fat, you can consult your vet and consider changing the amount of food given.

Any time you switch a dog to a new food, it is best to do it slowly so as not to upset the animal's gastrointestinal tract. I usually manage the transition over a seven-day period. I start by mixing a tiny amount of the new food with the old food on the first day. Then, each successive day, I slightly increase the proportion of new food to old. By the seventh day, my Welsh has switched entirely to the new food. Throughout this

Photo Courtesy of Cindy Duber

process, I keep a close eye on my dog and its poop to make sure the diet change agrees with it.

Before you switch to a new dog food, do your research. There is an incredible array of puppy/dog food available, and it's difficult to choose. There are kibble, canned, fresh, raw, dehydrated, and human-grade foods produced for dogs, with a vast array of ingredients.

It's a good idea to check if a food meets the nutrition profile developed by the Association of American Feed Control Officials (AAFCO) for your dog's life stage. Also, you want food that lists whole meat or meat meal as the first ingredient. (Canned products may list water or broth as the first ingredients, but meat should follow.) Reading the list of ingredients in a dog food can be very eye-opening.

You should consider treats when calculating your pet's rations. For a Welsh, these tidbits should be small. (A large-dog biscuit is practically a meal for this breed without fully meeting its nutritional needs.) Limit the goodies to no more than 10% of your dog's daily diet. Everyone in the household needs to follow your terrier's regimen for treats and meals.

If you find yourself giving lots of food rewards during training, use a portion of your Welshie's actual dog food for treats if it is kibble. Or choose a very low-calorie treat like diced baby carrots or small bits of apple.

I don't recommend giving table scraps as treats. This encourages a dog to pester you when you're eating and may make it think it's entitled to your food. I also like to make my terriers work for any treats rather than just randomly giving them for no reason. This reinforces my position as leader.

If you are going to share your food with a Welsh Terrier, please remember that many human foods are dangerous for dogs. The typical American diet is too rich, fatty, and spicy for canines, and eating our foods can lead to gastrointestinal upset and even pancreatitis. Chocolate, avocados, coffee, tea, and anything sweetened with the artificial sweetener xylitol are a few foods that can be fatal to your pet. Cooked bones can splinter and pierce the gastrointestinal tract, so never give these to a Welshie. Ask your vet for more information about which human foods are dangerous to dogs.

For any Welsh Terrier with a hard-to-solve dietary issue, ask your vet for a referral to a veterinary nutritionist who is a diplomate of the American College of Veterinary Nutrition.

One important canine nutritional tool is a good probiotic. It's usually wise to give this to your dog during and after a course of antibiotics to help maintain a healthy gastrointestinal microbiome. (When your Welshie takes an antibiotic, it destroys the good bacteria in its gut as well as the bad.) There are numerous canine probiotics on the market, and they're useful to have in your terrier's nutritional arsenal. I encourage you to learn more about this dietary aid.

Whatever you feed your dog, make sure you pick a feeding location that is easy to clean and doesn't have a lot of foot traffic. Your Welshie should feel safe when eating. Also, remember that clean water should be available to your dog throughout the day.

Choosing a Vet & Other Professionals

It's a good idea to find the dog professionals you need before you bring your terrier home. Choosing a veterinarian is especially important. You should take your pet for a checkup during its first week with you. You'll also want the vet information just in case any health issues pop up.

To find a vet, think about what you and your Welshie will need. For an animal with health issues, look for a vet who is very experienced with that problem. The practice's location and hours should also be a consideration.

Getting recommendations is a good way to start your search. If the Welshie is coming from a local breeder or rescue, ask them to suggest a vet. Area dog owners, groomers, and trainers can also be wonderful sources of information.

Once you have some suggestions, go online and check out the different practices. Look at the location, hours, and services offered, and check out bios and accreditation. You want a vet that is close to you and who has hours that fit your normal schedule. You can read online reviews, but you should keep in mind that there will always be negative ones, regardless of the practice's quality. I have found it better to rely on recommendations from dog professionals and local owners than to pay too much attention to reviews. However, if the reviews are overwhelmingly bad, that is not a good sign.

Once you have narrowed down your list, call the practices you are considering. Ask how long it takes for a new client to get an appointment. (Ask the same question about regular clients.) You can also inquire about charges for regular checkups and vaccinations. If you are planning to schedule an appointment, they should be able to give you an estimate. Pay attention to the helpfulness and friendliness of the employee you speak with. If possible, visit the office to meet the staff and check out the environment.

As soon as you know your Welsh Terrier's arrival date, schedule a veterinary appointment for its first week with you. This will give your vet a chance to examine the dog, review health records, check for undiagnosed health issues, answer questions you may have, and set up a future schedule for the dog. Good veterinary practices are busy, so make the appointment before you get your pet. It's hard to get a regular appointment at the last minute.

If the veterinary clinic you choose is not a 24-hour service, ask them what emergency vet they send clients to when closed. Keep the emergency service information where you can find it in a hurry. If the dog eats something it shouldn't or has an accident after hours on its first night in your home, you don't want to waste time looking for emergency vet info.

Other professionals you may need include a dog walker/pet sitter, groomer, trainer, and boarding kennel. Whoever is placing the dog with you may be a wonderful source of information for these people. You can also ask your veterinarian for recommendations and talk to local dog owners about who they use and their experiences with them.

CHAPTER 5

Bringing Home Your Welsh Terrier

The Importance of Having a Plan

> *For the first few weeks (or months, with a puppy!), someone should always be watching the dog when it is not confined. This means truly watching, not watching TV or cooking or gardening, and learning about the dog through observation. While making sure that the dog does not get hurt or damage anything, this time can be used to figure out how the dog acts when it needs to go out, what it is interested in, and what it is likely to do when it is not as closely observed. This allows the family to make an appropriate plan for gradually and safely increasing the dog's access to more and more parts of the house.*
>
> **LUCY BAILEY**
> *WYSIWYG Welsh Terriers*

Having an advance plan for the supervision and management of your Welsh Terrier makes the dog's introduction into your home more likely to be successful.

Here are a few suggestions to ensure an easier adjustment for your new Welshie:

Chapter 5: Bringing Home Your Welsh Terrier

Photo Courtesy of Sheryl Azzam

Obtain the Essential Paperwork for Your Dog

- Signed and dated dog sales or placement contract between you and the breeder, rescue group, or shelter.
- AKC registration. This will be either a registration application for a puppy or a registration transfer for a dog that is already registered. These should be filled out by the breeder/previous owner and ready for you to submit to the AKC. (These forms can also be completed and submitted online through the AKC website.) I recommend submitting these forms to the AKC as soon as possible so that you don't forget. Adopted dogs don't come with registrations.
- Pedigree certificate that shows the most recent generations of your dog's family tree. Adopted dogs don't come with pedigrees.
- Microchip certificate if the dog is already chipped. You will want to change the contact information for the chip to your contact information as soon as possible.
- Veterinary documentation for your dog, including vaccination history, worming history, and a record of veterinary checkups and treatments. Your vet will want to see this information when you take the dog for its first checkup.

- Feeding instructions for the dog's current diet and the current schedule for feedings and activities.

A few additional items that are nice if you can get them include a few days supply of the dog's current food, an article scented by its canine buddies or a caregiver, and a list of command words the dog knows.

The Ride Home
- It's never safe to let a dog ride loose in any car. Your pet could interfere with your operation of the vehicle or become a projectile in a car accident. Secure your dog in a crate or with a seatbelt harness.
- If the dog isn't used to car rides, ask a friend or family member to accompany you on the drive. They can comfort the terrier and offer it treats while you do the driving.
- If possible, go straight home with no stops. You don't want to create extra anxiety for your Welshie by visiting more places than necessary.

At Home
- Take the dog to go potty as soon as you arrive home. (If you don't have a yard, you can take a fully vaccinated Welshie for a walk, but it's risky to walk in public places with a Welsh Terrier that's not fully vaccinated. I discuss house-training options for a dog that's not fully vaccinated in Chapter 6.) You want to show your new terrier where to go to the bathroom and give it a chance to relieve itself before taking it indoors. You'll also want to allow it extra time outdoors to burn off some energy before entering your home for the first time.
- Keep your new pet on a leash in a fenced yard until you are sure you can catch it.
- Keep your Welsh companion leashed inside your home initially as well. Once your new pet is comfortable and you can catch it, the leash can come off.
- Don't allow your Welsh Terrier the run of your home for the first week. On the first day, choose a room where you and your dog can relax together. This room is its "safe space." Gradually introduce the dog to the rest of your home as it settles in.

Chapter 5: Bringing Home Your Welsh Terrier

- Leave your new dog alone in its safe space for short periods, starting on day one. (You can gradually increase the time.) Don't create separation anxiety syndrome in your terrier by spending every minute with it at the beginning.
- Routine equals stability for canines. Immediately start introducing the dog to its new schedule.
- From day one, teach your Welsh Terrier the household rules. Don't confuse it by allowing certain behavior initially and then suddenly changing the rules.

It takes time for any dog to learn the routines of a new household. Expect some accidents and lapses, even with an adult Welshie. Just stay calm and watch for behaviors you can reward.

Introducing Your Human Family

With your Welsh Terrier on a leash, you can make introductions indoors or outdoors. Wherever you do this, be sure the dog has room to move away from someone if it wants to.

Introduce people one at a time rather than in an overwhelming crowd. Let your terrier choose whether to approach someone or not. Dogs don't like to be pursued by strangers. In fact, initially, if people ignore your dog, this may help ease any worries the animal has about a person. When your Welshie meets someone, let it sniff the person before being petted.

Photo Courtesy of Hayley Rampton

People should give the dog treats only when all four of its paws are on the floor. If your Welshie tends to raise its front paws and put them against people or even jump on them, have people drop treats on the floor rather than giving goodies by hand. (Be careful not to give too many treats. You don't want your new pet to have an upset tummy on the first day.)

It's important from the start to maintain a relaxed environment for your new Welshie. Everyone should speak in a calm voice and avoid roughhousing. Keep introductions to children low-key and quiet. Ask them not to run or move suddenly because this could excite or startle the dog. Also, make sure they use their inside voices around their new Welsh companion.

Once a Welsh Terrier seems relaxed and has sniffed a child, she or he can gently pet the dog around its shoulders and back. Petting is good; hugging and kissing a Welshie is not. Most important of all, be sure to always supervise young children with your dog.

If your new terrier gets excited or anxious, take it outside for a potty break and then put it in its safe space or crate with a chew toy for some downtime. Both adult dogs and puppies spend a lot of time napping, so make sure your dog has a chance to rest amid all the excitement.

Allow your Welsh Terrier a few days to settle in before inviting anyone over. If you plan to use a dog walker, be sure to introduce this person to your pet prior to the day he or she will care for it.

If There Is Already Another Dog at Home

> *I would recommend first introducing the dogs on leads in neutral territory and going for a walk. See how the dogs do, and when you decide to go home, go in together—but keep the leads on in case you need to separate the dogs for any reason. Be aware of guarding behavior so that you can nip it in the bud—keep food picked up and watch for any guarding of toys or people.*
>
> ELIZABETH BERRY
> *Airedale and Welsh Terrier Rescue*

Introduce your new Welsh Terrier to your current dog in a neutral location, like a park, where your current dog won't feel territorial. If the new dog hasn't completed its series of puppy vaccinations, a friend or neighbor's backyard would be fine for the first meeting.

This first meeting between your pets is going to require two people: one person for each dog. Both animals should be on a leash. To avoid sparking jealousy in your current dog, you will be the one holding its leash. The other person can hold the new dog's leash. Be prepared to praise and reward positive interactions between the dogs. You want this to be a good experience for both.

Don't immediately bring the dogs close to each other. Instead, walk parallel paths that allow the animals to see and scent each other in the air. When both dogs seem happy and interested in one another, you can slowly move them closer together until they meet. Let them sniff and interact for several minutes, and then start walking again. For at least a few times, you should alternate between walking the dogs and allowing them to interact.

If one dog becomes uncomfortable or tense, both need to be distracted and moved apart. Then the introduction can begin again, and you should take things a little more slowly. Whatever happens, don't scold or yell at either animal because one dog may associate that negative experience with the other dog.

Once the dogs seem happy and relaxed with each other, it's time to head home. Let the new dog enter your home first. This may prevent your old dog from trying to keep the new one out.

FAMOUS WELSH TERRIERS

Welshie in the White House

When John F. Kennedy became the 35th president of the United States, he brought his beloved Welsh Terrier, Charlie, to Washington, D.C. Charlie was the first Welsh Terrier to reside in the White House and had been a gift to the president from his wife during his campaign. Though JFK was reportedly allergic to dogs, he owned many canines throughout his life. Charlie enjoyed swimming laps with the president, playing fetch, and was known for being protective of JFK.

Photo Courtesy of Alyssa Teixeira

Carefully supervise all interactions between the dogs for at least the first few weeks. You don't want to allow either to become a nuisance or a bully to the other. Separate the dogs at the first sign that one is tense or unhappy with the other. Try not to yell at or scold either of the dogs when they are together.

If your new dog is a young puppy, don't be surprised if you hear your old dog growl when the pup forgets its manners. It's okay unless the old dog is trying to hurt the youngster. Older dogs help a puppy learn how to behave with other canines.

If a puppy gets too rambunctious or is an excessive pest with your other dog, give the pup a little exercise to calm it down. You can also try redirecting the pup's attention. If neither of those things works, try putting the puppy—without scolding— in short timeouts in a crate or x-pen.

This can help the youngster figure out it needs to play nicely. Don't wait until your older dog is completely fed up with the puppy before you act.

Separate the dogs to feed them and avoid giving them high-value treats or chews when they are together. (If your dog ranked treats and chews from one to ten where one is disliked and ten is wildly loved, high-value items would rate a ten. They're like chocolate to a chocoholic.)

Don't leave toys out in the beginning. When you do let the dogs have toys together, give them enough so that there is little chance of a quarrel over any particular toy.

Both dogs should get some one-on-one attention. Make sure the older one doesn't feel left out, and try to maintain its routine. Also, schedule quiet time for each dog. Canines have very individual personalities. You can't make them love each other or rush the relationship.

Introducing Your Cat

If you have a cat, you can give it something with the Welshie's scent on it, like a towel or old T-shirt at least a few days before your dog arrives. This will help the feline become familiar with the scent ahead of time. You can do the same thing in reverse for the terrier.

Once your Welsh Terrier arrives, keep the dog and cat in separate rooms initially. (See Chapter 4 for information on how to prepare their rooms) They should be able to smell and hear one another but not see each other. This is enough familiarization for the first day or so.

On the second day, while your Welshie is outside or shut up in another room, allow the cat to roam rooms the dog has occupied and get used to its smell in the house. Put the cat back in its room before bringing your terrier back. You want to prevent the animals from seeing one another until they are both relaxed and used to each other's smell.

For the first meeting, your Welsh Terrier should be leashed while the cat is allowed to roam freely. Let the feline choose how close it wants to get to the new member of the family. Encourage and reward the animals for any calm or positive behavior. If your Welshie becomes excited or aggressive, tell it to "leave it." Then distract it with a toy or some simple exercises like "sit," "look," or "spin." (Never allow the dog to chase the cat, even in play.) Keep this first meeting short.

Don't yell at the dog during this encounter. Yelling only escalates a situation, and the dog could blame the cat for being yelled at. Give commands calmly.

I do not recommend crating the dog for this meeting with your cat. A terrier may become frustrated and aggressive when confined to tight quarters as a strange feline roams freely nearby.

Gradually increase the number and length of meetings between the animals, keeping the dog leashed until their relationship seems solid. Always supervise interactions between dog and cat for at least the first few months. When no one can supervise, keep them separated.

If problems arise, try taking a step back and going slower. However, if the animals don't seem to get along, it is best to ask for help from your breeder or another expert before things get too out of hand.

Even after a dog and cat become friends or at least tolerant of each other, don't leave them alone in a room that doesn't have an escape route for the cat. I offer that advice for all canines, not just Welsh Terriers.

The speed at which this relationship develops depends on the individual animals. It could take weeks or even months for them to become comfortable with each other. For some, it never happens. A young Welsh Terrier is usually more capable of learning to live with a cat than an adult with no feline experience. Also, even a dog that grows to like its feline companion may need occasional reminders not to chase the cat.

I don't believe hunting or taking part in den trials makes Welsh Terriers more aggressive towards animals they already live with. They can understand the difference between the cat at home and a groundhog, rat, or fox in the field. In the March 2003 issue of Full Cry magazine, the "Working Airedale" column, usually devoted to that breed, contains a report of a Welsh Terrier named Roy hunting bears in Canada. According to its owner, Max Searls, this hunting terrier "doesn't bother the cats so long as they're in the house." Sadly, Roy has passed on since this column was published, but Searls has many wonderful memories of his Welsh buddy.

The First Night

There are a few things you can do prior to bedtime to help the night pass more smoothly:

- Remove the dog's water about an hour before bed so it doesn't tank up at the last minute.
- Try to feed a puppy its last meal of the day at least three hours before bed.
- Play gently with your dog prior to taking it potty before bedtime. A little exercise will burn off some energy. However, roughhousing may overstimulate your pet and make it more difficult for it to settle down.
- Make sure your terrier always goes potty shortly before bed. Not having a full bladder helps it sleep longer.

Prepare the sleeping area ahead of time. If you have a scented article from your Welshie's previous home, place it in the crate/bed. You can also provide a safe, age-appropriate chew toy for stress relief during the night. If you have a crate, let the dog see you toss a small treat inside before you ask the dog to enter. This helps teach it to like the crate. (You can also hide another small treat at the back of the crate for the dog to discover.) If you are not using a crate, I strongly advise you to place the bed inside a small, enclosed area or exercise pen with pee pads on the floor.

If your Welsh Terrier isn't used to spending the night in a crate, don't shut it in on the first night. That would traumatize the dog. Instead, put the crate, with the door open, inside a small pen. The dog can go into the crate to sleep but won't be shut in.

You have several choices regarding where you and your new pet sleep the first few nights:

- The Welsh Terrier will sleep in a crate or exercise pen in its safe space, which it got used to during the day, not your bedroom. You will sleep in your bedroom.
- The dog will sleep in a crate or exercise pen in your bedroom. Having you nearby so it can smell and hear you may be comforting to your Welshie. If you don't want the terrier in your bedroom in the future, you can gradually move the dog out after it settles in.

- Your Welshie can sleep in a crate or exercise pen in its safe space, not your bedroom, while you temporarily sleep on a nearby couch.

I don't recommend letting your terrier sleep in your bed initially, even if you are going to allow it later. The first few weeks with a new dog are about teaching boundaries. Once your pet has learned what its space is and what your space is, you can invite it into your bed. Whatever the sleeping arrangements, you can always adjust or move things if it's not working out.

Don't be surprised if your dog whines or cries on the first few nights before it settles in and goes to sleep. Don't take it out of its crate or bed to cuddle when this happens. That would reward the whining and crying behavior. If you are in the same room, you can calmly tell the dog "quiet" or "easy," reminding it you're there. If the crate is close enough, you can gently rest your hand on the crate to give assurance that you are close. Other than that, just try to ignore the noise unless it continues for a long time.

If your Welsh continues making noise nonstop or suddenly cries in the middle of the night, it may need to go potty. (Stress can sometimes cause even adult dogs to need a bathroom break during the night.) Take it outside. Then, praise and give it a treat when it goes to the bathroom. Beyond the reward, don't play with or talk to the dog. Afterward, quietly return the dog to its bed/crate. If you cuddle or play with it instead, you will be teaching it to expect that every night.

A young puppy may need several potty breaks during the night. If you aren't willing to take it out in the middle of the night or don't think you'll hear its cries, don't lock the pup in a crate. (You don't want it to get used to using a crate as a potty.) Instead, let it sleep in an open crate placed inside an exercise pen with pee pads on the floor of the pen.

As a puppy matures, it will need to go potty fewer and fewer times during the night. Eventually, it will be able to sleep through the night without a potty break. If you have another dog, it may be better for the animals to sleep in different rooms until they are comfortable with each other.

In the morning, don't make a fuss over the Welsh Terrier when you release it from its crate or pen. Just take the dog outside to potty right away and reward it when it goes.

Chapter 5: Bringing Home Your Welsh Terrier

The first couple of nights are usually the most difficult. It gets easier as your Welshie learns the schedule (and physically matures if it's a puppy) and you learn what it needs.

First Vet Visit

Your new Welsh Terrier should visit the vet during the first week. In fact, some breeders' contracts require a new owner to have their dog examined by a vet within the first 72 hours of bringing it home. Hopefully, you scheduled an appointment as soon as you knew your dog's arrival date. (Last-minute vet examinations are not always available.) You will find information in Chapter 4 on preselecting a veterinarian before bringing your dog home.

Photo Courtesy of Mary Duafala

I prefer to let a pet settle into its new home for at least one day before visiting the vet. That gives you a chance to begin to know the animal and notice if it's experiencing any issues, such as stress-related diarrhea.

There are a few things you should take to your dog's first vet visit:

- Any medical records and other relevant information you received with the dog.
- A poop sample that's as fresh as possible.
- The names of any medication your Welshie is on.
- Information about the dog's food and treats.
- A list of questions/concerns to discuss with the vet. If you have a list, you won't forget something you wanted to discuss.
- Treats to keep your dog happy in the waiting and exam rooms. (A chew toy, if you plan to keep it in a crate until the exam.)
- A leash and collar/harness, even if you are carrying your pet inside with a crate.

If this is a very young puppy, keep it inside a crate in the waiting room or wait in the car with it to prevent contact with other animals. (I like to notify the practice when I arrive with a puppy that's not fully vaccinated and then wait in the car until the exam room is ready.) The vet will require you to fill out a new patient information form. If you can, do this online ahead of the visit.

Don't let your dog pester other animals in the reception area. You don't know what medical issues they have, and some pets get nervous in a vet's office and aren't in the mood to play. Instead, shower your dog with attention. Ask it to do simple things like "sit" or "look" and give rewards. Speak to your terrier calmly during the visit. You don't want this to be an unpleasant experience.

The vet will review your Welsh Terrier's medical records and conduct a physical exam, checking the heart, lungs, ears, eyes, mouth, and more. They'll determine the dog's current state of health, which will provide a good baseline for the future. They'll talk to you about any medical issues noted and how to maintain your pet's health. Vaccinations should be discussed, as well as the prevention of heartworms, ticks, fleas, and intestinal parasites. (We'll take a look at healthcare issues in Chapter 8.)

Some topics you may want to discuss include:

- Spaying/neutering
- Dental health
- Diet
- Toy safety
- Microchipping
- Pet insurance
- Schedule for vaccinations and follow-up appointments

Before you leave, set up appointments for any vaccinations and/or follow-up exams suggested by the vet. Make sure you understand the directions for any prescribed medications. Also, keep the paperwork from this visit with the rest of your dog's medical records.

Puppy Classes

The optimal time for socializing a puppy ends by the age of 16 weeks. Until then, it soaks up life experiences like a sponge, curious to investigate and happy to accept all sorts of things as normal. After that age, "new" may be met with a certain amount of suspicion instead of curiosity.

That is why kindergarten/puppy classes are important. They allow a puppy to safely experience a variety of people, other puppies, and new objects, surfaces, and sounds. In fact, a major aim of these classes is socialization. The class will also teach you how to handle and train your puppy, prevent behavioral problems, and deal with those problems if they arise.

According to the American Veterinary Society of Animal Behavior (AVSAB), "Puppies should receive a minimum of one set of vaccines at least 7 days prior to the first class and a first deworming. They should be kept up to date on all vaccines throughout the class."

To help your puppy stay safe, look for the following things in a puppy class:

- A vaccine requirement: The training facility should require all dogs and puppies to be up to date on vaccinations. Instructors should ask for proof of vaccination.
- The floor should have been disinfected before each puppy class.
- Puppy owners should be asked to disinfect their shoes or wear protective shoe covers during class.

Your local kennel club can be a great resource for information about classes in your area. When you've located a class, check a trainer's references and/or check their certification from a training organization/school.

If possible, watch a class to see how it's managed. Make sure that puppies are trained using positive reinforcement. They should be having fun and be enthusiastic about training. If playtime is offered, it should be divided by size, and bossy puppies should not be allowed to bully shyer puppies. A good instructor understands dog body language and closely supervises puppy play. Watch out for playgroups that are so large as to be unmanageable. Puppies should not be over 16 weeks old by the end of this series of classes.

When taking a class, make sure your puppy goes potty before you leave home and carry it from the car into the training room. If your pup needs a potty break during class, look for a spot away from the building not frequented by other dogs.

Toy Safety

Dogs love and need toys, and you need to make sure those toys are safe. The four major concerns with dog toys are:

- Choking
- Ingestion of nondigestibles
- Toxins
- Tooth Damage

To avoid a choking hazard, choose the right size toys for your dog. You want a toy that is too big to go into the back of your Welshie's mouth or be swallowed. The correct size toy will change as a puppy grows to its adult size.

Watch out for toys or toy parts that a dog could tear/chew off and then choke on or ingest. Sometimes you can pull or cut off eyes, ribbons, or other parts to make a toy safe. With rope toys, supervise play and watch that the strings are not being chewed off. For aggressive rope chewers, it's probably best not to give dogs these toys at all.

I used to give my dogs rawhide chews. Then one of my Welshies broke off a sizeable piece of rawhide that got stuck in the very back of its mouth, and I had to pry it out. It could have been worse. It could have gotten stuck in the dog's esophagus. I stopped giving my dogs rawhide chews after that.

Some chew toys require proper supervision. For example, I always watch my Welshies when they are chomping on a bully stick. Before a terrier has chewed the stick small enough to swallow whole, I take it away. This chew toy is digestible, but it could become lodged in a dog's throat if the Welshie tries to swallow a large enough piece.

Welsh Terriers love to destroy toys and pull out the innards. For that reason, I always look for toys that are indestructible and supervise play if necessary. (For many Welshies, there is no such thing as an indestructible toy, but so-called indestructible toys last longer.) You should remove any toy that shows some wear and tear before your pet rips it open. My dogs loved to destroy squeaky toys, but proper supervision allowed them to enjoy these beloved noise-makers safely.

Photo Courtesy of Sheryl Azzam

Dog toys aren't regulated as well as children's toys, so some canine toys may contain dangerous levels of substances like lead, phthalates, or toxic dyes. Even some rawhide chews are processed with unhealthy chemicals. If a toy has a strong chemical odor, don't buy it. You can and should check where it is made, but being manufactured in the United States doesn't guarantee a toy is nontoxic. Check online to see if a toy brand has produced toxic toys in the past or if people are currently encountering problems.

Veterinary dentists usually warn against chew toys like cow hooves, antlers, and bones because they can damage or break a dog's teeth. However, I must admit to occasionally giving a raw bone as a special treat. Never give cooked bones to a dog because they can splinter. Even chewing on the outer fuzz of a tennis ball can wear down a dog's tooth enamel. It's okay for a dog to play fetch under supervision with the right-sized ball, but don't let it chew on that fuzz.

CHAPTER 6

House-training Your Welsh Terrier

> *At first, you will need to watch the puppy carefully for signs that he wants to go out. Always take the puppy out after a meal, and first and last thing every morning and evening. Make sure to praise the puppy when he goes potty outside! When no one is home, the puppy should be crated as part of his potty training because puppies will generally not go potty in their crates.*
>
> ELIZABETH BERRY
> *Airedale and Welsh Terrier Rescue*

In my experience, Welsh Terriers try very hard to go to the bathroom where you want them to go once they understand what you want. Unless they have a medical issue, most dogs can be house-trained with proper management, supervision, patience, and positive reinforcement.

The Importance of Routine

A regular schedule for three things will make house-training much easier:

1. Feed your Welsh Terrier on a schedule and remove uneaten food after twenty minutes. This will help the dog poop on a fairly regular schedule and make house-training easier. If you free-feed your dog,

it may eat and poop throughout the day, and house-training will be more difficult.
2. Scheduled potty breaks, geared to the needs of your Welshie, help it avoid accidents in the house and learn to rely on people to take it potty when it needs to go. Initially, these bathroom breaks should be on leash.
3. Exercising around the same time every day can help a dog eliminate with more regularity because it aids gastrointestinal motility.

Supervision during House-training

Besides a routine, your Welshie needs supervision during house-training. Monitoring your dog allows you to notice when it needs to go out (besides your scheduled potty breaks) and know if it actually goes to the bathroom when you take it outside.

Individual Welsh Terriers show different signals when they need to go potty, and you will gradually learn your dog's tip-offs. Some common signs that a dog needs to go potty include circling, whining, sniffing around, and restlessness. (You don't want to watch/wait for a sign from a very young puppy because they have little bladder or bowel control.) If your Welshie shows signs of needing a potty break, don't yell at it. Yelling could teach your dog not to signal and to instead potty when you aren't looking. Instead, put the leash on your Welsh Terrier and take it to its potty spot as quickly as possible.

You always want to watch and make sure your dog goes to the bathroom when you take it outside to the potty spot, even if you have a fenced yard. If the dog doesn't go after five minutes, take it back inside and keep it with you and on leash. After ten minutes (or sooner if the dog signals), take the dog outside again. Keep repeating these steps until you see the dog go potty. Remember not to take your eyes off your Welshie when you bring it back inside unless you confine it to a crate or small area.

Young puppies may need to urinate more than once to empty their bladder. Don't rush back inside after your Welshie pees one time. Instead, wait at least a few more moments to give the youngster a chance to urinate again if it needs to.

Photo Courtesy of Rhonda Metcalf.

When you can't supervise a dog during house-training, it should be confined. Make sure your dog has recently gone to the bathroom before confining it in a crate, x-pen, or small enclosed area. How long you should crate your Welshie during the day for house-training depends on how long it can hold its urine. Every dog is a little different, and you will gradually learn how often your new Welsh Terrier needs to pee.

If you must confine your dog for longer than it can wait to use the bathroom, don't shut it in a crate. Instead, arrange for someone to take your dog potty while you are away from home. If that is not an option, you can leave your terrier in a small space with a crate/bed, toys, and water/food bowls on one side and pee pads on the other side.

If you have trouble tracking your dog's activities or there are multiple people caring for it, keep a diary of your dog's activities and when it relieves its bladder and bowels. This will help you develop a sense of your Welshie's natural rhythms and allow you to adjust the dog's schedule if necessary.

You also should clean up any indoor potty accidents with a nontoxic, enzymatic cleaner to remove the odor. (You can find enzymatic cleaners in pet supply stores.) Otherwise, the smell will attract your dog and lead it to use that spot as an indoor bathroom again.

Positive Reinforcement

The key to house-training is watching and rewarding your dog for going potty where you want it to go. This is much easier than retraining a dog after it learns the wrong lesson from being yelled at/punished for going to the bathroom in the wrong place or being left unsupervised to go potty in the house.

Whenever your Welsh Terrier goes to the bathroom outside, you want to praise and reward the dog with a treat as soon as it finishes. Sometimes the reward can include playtime or a fun walk after the dog has done its business. These potty parties help your dog understand where you want it to go potty.

Positive reinforcement works much better than negative reinforcement. If you yell at a dog or punish it for an accident in the house, you may teach your Welshie not to go potty in front of you. That will make house-training much more difficult.

Years ago, I acquired an adult Welsh Terrier bitch who would not go potty when I was watching. If I put her in a crate for just a few minutes, she would go potty in the crate. (This poor dog would rather foul her crate than go potty in front of a person.) My mother, a long-time Irish Terrier breeder, advised me to keep my dog on leash and under close supervision until this problem was solved. To help overcome this Welshie's fear, my mom suggested taking the dog outside on a 15-foot-long line and letting her go to the end while I pretended not to watch.

My terrier finally went to the bathroom outside on the long line, and I praised and gave her treats as soon as she finished. After repeating this a few more times, this Welsh Terrier learned to go potty outside on leash in front of a person.

If you catch your terrier in the act of peeing or pooping in the house, you can calmly clap your hands and say something like, "Hey, you." You don't want to yell or sound angry. You just want to startle the dog enough to interrupt what it is doing. Then you can gently scoop your dog up and carry it outside to potty. (If you are close to the terrier, you can pick it up while it is going potty and carry it outside. That should be startling enough to make your dog stop in the middle of going potty.) When you return, you can clean the site of the accident.

If you don't catch your dog in the act but find pee or poo in the house, just clean up the mess. Don't reprimand the dog because it won't understand that it is being yelled at for something that happened previously.

Where a Dog Goes Potty

The goal is to teach your Welsh Terrier to use the bathroom outdoors and hold its pee and poop when it's indoors. Since dogs like to use the bathroom where they've gone before, house-training will be easier if you take your dog to the same spot every time. Your Welshie will begin to recognize the visual and scent cues of this potty spot and understand what you expect when you take it there. You also must remove the odor when cleaning any spot your dog has an accident in the house so that scent cues don't cause the dog to recognize that spot as its indoor bathroom.

If your dog can't go outside often enough and sometimes must go potty indoors on pee pads (or another alternative potty aid), house-training your Welsh Terrier may take longer. It's confusing for a dog to go potty inside sometimes and outside other times. Eventually, house-training your Welshie will require that someone spend time with the dog and bear responsibility for supervising it, taking it outside often enough to avoid indoor accidents, and rewarding it for doing its business outside. That is the only way to teach a dog to go potty reliably outside.

If you don't have a private yard, I recommend waiting until a puppy has all its puppy shots

> **FUN FACT**
>
> **The Canine Muse: Tomie dePaola's WT Connection**
>
> Did you know that Tomie dePaola, renowned children's author and illustrator, had a special bond with Welsh Terriers? These delightful dogs played a significant role in his life and even influenced his work. Tomie shared his home with several Welsh Terriers throughout the years, and their playful antics and spirited personalities inspired some of his beloved characters and illustrations. This connection with the breed showcased his deep appreciation for their loyalty, intelligence, and undeniable charm, leaving an indelible paw print in both his heart and his creative endeavors.

to bring it home from the breeder. (We'll take a closer look at vaccinations in Chapter 8.) If you end up with a young Welshie that hasn't finished its vaccinations and you don't have a yard, ask your veterinarian about the risk of disease in your area so you can weigh the threat to your puppy. If the disease rate is very low, you could carry your pup to an outdoor potty spot not frequented by other dogs and then carry it back inside. Your youngster will need to avoid not only other dogs that may be unvaccinated but also their urine and poop. Otherwise, you will need to set up an indoor potty for your Welsh Terrier until it's fully vaccinated.

Exposure to other dogs isn't an issue when house-training a fully vaccinated dog or even with a not completely vaccinated pup in a private, fenced-in yard. For these dogs, the best potty area during house-training is one without too many distractions. This will allow your Welshie to concentrate on doing its business while learning bathroom etiquette.

The Puppy

In general, a puppy can hold its urine a maximum of about an hour for every month of its age. It's best to take a puppy out before it has held its urine for the maximum time. (A pup can hold it longer at night when asleep.) This one-hour-for-every-month-of-age rule is just for a very young dog who doesn't yet have an adult-sized bladder. Please don't expect a healthy adult terrier to hold its urine for over six to eight hours because of this puppy rule.

Additional times when a young puppy needs to go potty include:

- when it wakes up in the morning
- after naps
- after eating and/or drinking
- after play/exercise or any excitement
- just before bed
- during the night

As your puppy matures, the size of its bladder and bowels increases, and it can go longer between potty breaks. You may notice this and adjust your Welshie's schedule accordingly.

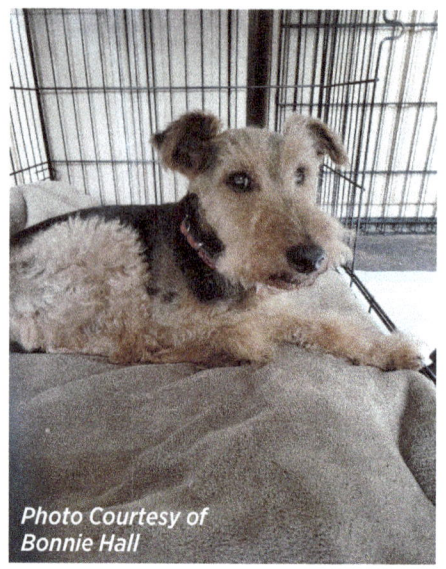
Photo Courtesy of Bonnie Hall

Every individual puppy is different. If your Welsh puppy is having accidents in the house, it could mean it needs to go out more often to relieve itself. If your youngster doesn't go potty on some of its trips outside, that may mean it's maturing and can wait a little longer to go out. Keeping a diary of your pup's activities and bowel and bladder movements will help you tailor the schedule to your youngster's needs.

If you don't notice any changes as your puppy matures, you can try stretching out the time between potty breaks by an extra five to ten minutes. When your Welsh Terrier can handle that, stay with the new schedule for a week and then try stretching the time out a little more. Should your pup have trouble with added time between potty breaks, take a step back to what worked. Then try again in a week.

After a puppy has gone two to three months without having an accident in the house, you can gradually allow it a little more unsupervised freedom indoors. If house-training is consistent and started early, a puppy may be reliably house-trained by the time it is six months old. Every pup's rate of progress will be different, but with proper management and positive reinforcement, you can house-train a healthy Welsh Terrier puppy.

As previously mentioned in this chapter, and because it is extremely important, I recommend that people without access to a private yard wait until a Welsh Terrier pup is fully vaccinated to bring it home. A puppy is not considered completely protected against certain fatal, contagious diseases until its puppy series of vaccinations is finished, so taking a puppy out to potty in public spaces before that can be risky.

The Adult

A healthy adult Welsh Terrier can usually hold its urine for six to eight hours—but don't assume it can or will do this in the beginning. If you are adopting a dog from a foster home, find out about its potty schedule and try to keep it on a similar schedule with a few extra bathroom breaks initially. If you don't know the dog's history or it's not housebroken, take it potty six or seven times for the first few days after you bring it home. Then you can adjust the schedule as you learn your dog's requirements.

An adult Welsh Terrier that has never been house-trained will need to learn to control its elimination and may initially require more potty breaks than a dog that is being re-house-trained. Even if your new dog is fully house-trained, manage, supervise, and offer positive reinforcement during the first week to help the Welshie adjust to a new environment and schedule.

To house-train an adult dog, you will employ the same method used to train a puppy. An adult may learn quicker than a puppy because of its physical maturity, but training could still take at least a couple of months. If a dog has developed a strong habit of going potty in the house, it takes even more time to untrain bad potty habits and teach new behavior.

Once your dog understands where you want it to go potty, is not having indoor accidents, and is reliable with its potty schedule, slowly increase the space your Welshie can access indoors while watching from a distance. If an accident happens, just take a step back in the house-training process. Eventually, your dog should be able to roam freely and unsupervised throughout your home without having accidents.

Most healthy adult Welsh Terriers will require about four trips outside to potty each day once they've settled in. If your dog seems to go potty too often, consult with a veterinarian about potential health issues.

An elderly dog will probably need to go out more often than a younger adult, as its bladder may have weakened with age. It's not unusual for a senior dog to need a bathroom break every four to six hours. Keeping a potty diary will help you figure out the needs of a senior Welshie.

Photo Courtesy of Tamara Pongers

Marking

All dogs use urine to give social signals and mark their territory; it's called marking. I have never had an issue with a house-trained dog marking in the house. If this is an issue, the dog is not fully house-trained, and you should continue potty training with the necessary management, supervision, and positive reinforcement for urinating outside. For a male dog that has a strong habit of marking indoors, try keeping a belly band on the dog when inside the house as you work to teach it to only mark outdoors.

Urine marking may seem a spiteful action to us humans, but it isn't. The scent of urine doesn't disgust dogs like it does us. Canines actually sniff other dogs' urine to read the pee-mail. They even have a special organ, the vomeronasal organ, in their nasal cavity for decoding the messages of pheromones in urine.

A dog can leave a variety of messages with its urine, including:

- Perimeter marking
- Reproductive status
- Excitement
- Ownership
- Stress
- Submission
- Fear

Try to figure out what message your terrier is conveying by marking in the house. Is it marking its territory or favorite property because a new pet is in the house? Is it excited over houseguests? Or is it stressed because its routine has been disrupted? Depending on the reason for urine marking, you may help stop it by dealing with the underlying cause.

Potty on Command

It's possible to teach your dog to go potty on command. This is handy when you are traveling or in a hurry. For starters, I suggest you choose a command word that is not too common. Accidents can happen with this command if your dog hears you say the word by mistake in the house.

To teach this command, softly say the word each time the dog begins to pee or poop. You don't want to say it too loud because that might startle the dog and cause it to stop going to the bathroom. As soon as your dog finishes peeing or pooping, praise and reward. The praise should include the command word. For instance, if your command is "peepoo," you should say "good peepoo." Gradually your dog will learn to associate the command with going potty. Eventually, you can give the command before the dog starts going to the bathroom, and they will respond.

Some people believe you should use different words for urination and defecation. I use the same word for both, and my dogs seem to understand. You can also teach a dog to ring a bell when it wants to go potty. Once the dog has mastered this trick, you'll be the one following the command of the bell.

Pee Pads and Other Indoor Potty Alternatives

I believe that having a dog use the bathroom inside can confuse it during house-training. However, there are situations where you may want an indoor pee station. Those include:

- You work during the day and can't arrange for a dog walker.
- You live in a high-rise apartment more than three floors up with a young pup or senior dog that needs to go out often.
- You don't have a private yard for an unvaccinated puppy.
- There is temporary extreme weather.

I suggest an indoor dog potty be located within a small, confined space or x-pen. You can either place the dog there when it needs to potty (and remove it afterward) or leave it in this space when you aren't able to take it out. If you plan to leave the dog in there for any length of time, place a bed/crate, food and water dishes, and toys on the opposite side of the space from the potty.

For a potty spot, you have the options of pee pads, paper, and dog potties with artificial or real turf. Pee pads created for dogs are often scented to encourage a dog to go to the bathroom on them. (If using unscented material, you can dab a paper towel in a puddle of your dog's urine and transfer that scent by wiping the wet paper towel on the material you want the dog to use as a potty. This will encourage your terrier to use the bathroom where the scent is located.) Some pee pads have adhesive on the back to help secure them to the floor, which can be helpful.

Sometimes, dogs treat pee pads like chew toys and shred them. For this problem, you can try spraying the edges with something to deter chewing. You could also consider bed pads made for incontinent humans that are washable and perhaps less shreddable. No matter what option you choose, expect some pee and poop on the floor. Dogs don't aim well.

When teaching your dog to go potty outside after it's been allowed to go inside, you may need to take the indoor potty material outdoors to convey that the bathroom has moved. Once you don't need the indoor potty, remove it and either keep the dog out of that area temporarily or place furniture or something else where the potty used to be.

Crate Training

Photo Courtesy of Patricia Mast

With the proper introduction, your Welsh Terrier can learn to enjoy spending time in a crate. This tool is handy for house-training, travel, and emergencies. A crate provides a safe place to confine your dog and should NEVER be used for punishment.

If your dog is not used to being crated, it is fairly easy to teach it to feel safe in one. First, place the crate (with the door removed or open) in a room where the dog hangs out with you. You can put a few toys or cookies around the crate to encourage the dog to investigate the area. Give the dog some time to explore the crate on its own. Your Welshie may go in and out of the crate with no coaxing.

If your dog is worried, you can try sitting beside the crate as you play with your dog and give it treats. Don't force your Welshie into the crate. You can toss a cookie or toy into the front of the crate for your dog to reach in and grab. Try to act nonchalant.

Once your dog is comfortable reaching into the front of the crate to grab a treat or a toy, toss these goodies further into the crate. Eventually, you want your dog to go all the way to the back of the crate to get its prize. Don't close the crate at this point; instead, allow the dog to enter and leave as it pleases.

After the dog seems comfortable going in and out of the open crate, start feeding it in the crate with the door open. You may have to start with the food dish placed toward the middle of the crate. Over time, you can place the dish further into the crate until it is all the way at the back.

Once the dog is comfortable eating in the open crate, you can close the door while your Welshie eats and then open the door as soon as the dog is done eating. Gradually increase the time the door remains closed after your terrier finishes dinner to about ten minutes. If your dog gets

Photo Courtesy of Viktoria Ginzery

anxious or whines, take a step back in the process and go slower. (Before releasing a whining dog, try dropping a treat into the crate to distract your terrier from the door opening. You don't want to teach that whining causes the crate to open.) If your dog continues to be anxious, no matter how slow you go, you can try placing a high-value chew toy inside the crate along with your dog's dinner.

When comfortable eating dinner and then spending time in the crate, your Welsh Terrier is ready to stay a few minutes in the crate while you are nearby. Standing beside the crate, call your dog over and let it see you toss a treat into the crate as you give a command such as "crate" or "kennel." (This teaches your dog to enter its crate on command.) You can give your dog another treat once it's inside and then close the crate.

In the beginning, hang out near the crate so your presence reassures the dog. I like to place a chew toy in the crate beforehand to help the dog settle down. Gradually increase the time your dog is in the crate. Next, try leaving the room for a few minutes while your dog is crated, and then slowly increase how long you are gone. If everything goes well, your dog should be ready to stay crated for short periods while you leave the house. Gradually your dog will work up to staying in the crate for a few hours.

Eventually, your dog will be ready to try spending the night in a crate. If your dog cries during the night, take it outside to potty and then put it back in the crate without playing or cuddling. Stress from a new situation, such as being crated overnight, can cause even an adult dog to need a potty break. Make sure you can hear your dog if it cries during the night when it's learning to sleep in a crate.

There is no rule for how long crate training should take. Every dog is different. Some learn to relax and sleep in their crate in seven days. With other dogs, it can take weeks before they feel secure in their crate. The dog must dictate the speed of this process, but having a crate-trained dog is well worth the time and effort and is very useful when house-training.

CHAPTER 7

Grooming Your Welsh Terrier

The Welsh Terrier Coat

A Welsh Terrier grows two types of hair: the wire outer hair that gives the dog its color and the softer, woolly undercoat that may be a lighter shade than the topcoat. A Welshie's coat never reaches a stage where dead hairs fall out or shed in massive amounts. Not that you won't find a little hair on the floor or that a Welshie's coat won't grow into a matted, shaggy mess without proper coat maintenance.

Brushing

Welsh Terriers require brushing and combing once or twice a week to prevent mats and remove dead hair. Brushing also distributes natural oils throughout the coat and removes dust and debris.

I recommend the following equipment for brushing and combing your Welsh Terrier:

Soft slicker brush.
Comb through the coat with this brush to remove the undercoat, dead hair, and any tangles. Even though this slicker is "soft," you want to use it gently. Do not press down hard with it because it can scratch the dog's skin if you are not careful. I only use this tool on the neck, back, sides of the torso, and upper thighs of a dog.

Pin brush.

This brush has metal pins blunted at the ends that are long enough to get through both the wire hair and the undercoat. While not as powerful as the slicker brush, it can be used instead of the slicker if a dog is regularly brushed. You can use this brush over the entire dog. Just remember to be gentle in sensitive areas like the belly and face.

Terrier palm pad.

This oval-shaped brush with densely packed, short, blunted steel pins is great for tidying the furnishings. (The furnishings refer to the hair on the legs, the eyebrows, and the whiskers of a Welsh Terrier.) This brush also removes undercoat (when the jacket is not too long) and dead wire hair. While the palm pad is not as likely to scratch the skin as the slicker brush, you should still be gentle with this brush. It's a nice splurge for a terrier but not a necessity.

Seven-inch metal comb with teeth spaced widely at one end and narrowly at the other end.

This is sometimes called a greyhound comb. This comb is great for finding and taking out little tangles that might remain hidden. I usually start with the wide-toothed end and then go over the dog again with the narrow-toothed end of the comb.

Stiff bristle brush.

This is a great finishing brush for removing any remaining dirt/dust and loose hair. It also helps put a shine on your dog's coat by spreading the natural oils throughout it. I use this brush on my Welshies every day, and they love it.

For brushing and combing, you don't need a grooming table. Your dog should enjoy these grooming sessions, so the extra restraint isn't

HELPFUL TIP
The Perfect Brush

Welsh Terriers are hypoallergenic dogs with a non-shedding coat of hair. A unique feature of this breed's coat is its waterproof nature, resulting from a double coat capable of repelling moisture. This unique coat requires some special attention to avoid matting between layers. Some of the best tools for your Welshie's fur are a slicker brush, a pin brush, and a metal comb. Using these three tools, you can detangle, remove dead hair, and unpick any pesky knots or mats.

necessary. If your dog isn't used to being groomed, start slowly with brief periods of brushing and plenty of praise and treats. For a young puppy, start with short sessions using only the bristle brush.

You want to brush and comb in the direction the hair grows—except on the legs. You can use the palm pad, pin brush, and comb both with and against the direction of the hair on the legs to make sure you get out any little knots and fluff the furnishings.

Regular brushing and combing keep a Welsh Terrier's skin healthy and its coat shiny and mat free. These sessions are also a great time to check your dog's body for any new lumps, skin irritations, or cuts.

Stripping vs. Clipping

> *Welsh Terriers do not shed but need regular grooming to maintain their unique appearance and healthy coat. Hand stripping is used to maintain the hard, wiry coat typical of the breed. Their coat can also be clippered, though that does change the texture. Most professional groomers can do an okay job on a Welsh Terrier, but it is not that difficult for a motivated owner to learn.*
>
> **EREIGN SEACORD**
> *Esty Glen Welsh Terriers*

There are three ways to trim your Welsh Terrier's coat to keep it neat and tidy. You can learn to do any of these trimming methods yourself, or you can have your dog trimmed professionally. For all three methods, you will need a grooming table. Just remember to NEVER leave your dog unattended on the table. A dog can very quickly slip off or leap off a grooming table and wind up strangled by the noose. It is much safer to take your dog off the table for a few minutes when you can't pay attention.

The trimming method used for dogs that you see in the conformation show ring is called stripping, and it is very labor intensive. Stripping involves pulling the dead hairs out of the coat rather than cutting the hair. You either use a stripping knife or your fingers to grasp a few hairs at a time and pull them out.

If you want to learn how to strip your Welsh Terrier, ask your breeder or another terrier expert to teach you. Sometimes, terrier clubs hold grooming seminars where you can learn the art. Many years ago, I attended a grooming seminar put on by the Garden State All Terrier Club in New Jersey, where long-time Welsh Terrier breeder C. Freeman Ayers instructed us about Welsh Terrier grooming. It was a wonderful experience.

I highly recommend getting a copy of *Grooming the Broken-Coated Terrier* if you want to learn how to strip. This small book contains a series of articles by Arden Ross explaining how to strip a terrier and mainly focuses on Wire Fox Terriers. The information is useful for all wire-coated terriers, and you can tweak these directions to better suit a Welsh Terrier if you know the breed differences. This book is available for purchase on the Airedale Terrier Club of America's website (https://airedale.org/shopping/brochures-newsletter/grooming-the-broken-coated-terrier/). It is the best-written instruction for stripping a terrier that I have ever read.

A second method of trimming your Welsh Terrier is clipping. It's an easy way to maintain a tidy coat and show off the beautiful lines of your Welshie. Because it cuts the wire hairs and the undercoat to the same length, clipping changes the texture and color of a Welsh Terrier's coat to varying degrees. For instance, when a Welshie has lots of gray in its undercoat, clipping will make the gray more prominent. Also, a clipped coat is not weatherproof and may require bathing a little more often than a stripped coat.

You will need a clipper and clipper blades. I have always used an Oster A-5 clipper.

The blades I suggest are the #10 blade for the head, ears, neck, and butt. Depending on the season, you can use a #7, #10, or #5 for the body. The #10 blade leaves approximately one-sixteenth inch of hair, the #7 leaves one-eighth inch, and the #5 leaves one-fourth inch.

Note: Before clipping, brush and comb your Welsh Terrier thoroughly. You want to eliminate any little knots and brush off any dirt and dust.

Photo Courtesy of Mac Slobodien

Chapter 7: Grooming Your Welsh Terrier

Clipper blades get hot during clipping. When this happens (and it will), you can either give your dog a break while the blade cools off or use a special spray coolant on the blade. Overheated clipper blades can burn your dog's skin, so check your blades often when clipping.

You will also need scissors and thinning shears. I use my scissors for precise work, such as the foot pads and the edges of the ears. The type of thinning shears I use are primarily for blending and have teeth on one blade, and the other blade is solid.

You must always be very careful when using scissors or thinning shears on your dog's face. Keep the tips facing away from the eyes. If your Welshie suddenly tosses its head, you don't want to accidentally stab the dog's eye because the tip end was pointed toward it.

Clip in the direction the hair grows. Place your blade against the hair you are trimming and slowly let the hair feed into the trimmer as you gently push the clipper forward. You don't want to press the clipper down or push it forward with a lot of force.

The body, tail (top and sides), and part of the chest and neck (outlined as area 1 on the Illustration) can be clipped with a #7 blade when the weather is moderate. For summer heat, clip this area with a #10 blade. For cold winter weather, I suggest clipping this area with the #5 blade.

The forehead, cheeks, ears, and part of the neck comprise area 2 in the diagram. Use a #10 blade here. Imagine a line from the outside corner of the eye to the outside corner of the mouth and clip from that line back toward the neck. Under the jaw, you can clip a bit past the outside corner of the lip. I like to leave about half to three-quarters of the area under the bottom lip unclipped. (The unclipped bottom lip hair will end up shaped into a goatee. It is not a full beard.) You can clip the forehead from an area just behind where the eyebrows start and clip back toward the ears and neck in the direction of the hair growth.

After you have clipped the inside and outside of the ears, use your scissors to trim the outer edge of the ears evenly. Hold the ear in your hand and keep the scissors parallel to the edge. Be very careful not to cut the skin. As a precaution, you can place your fingers on either side of the skin's edge where you are cutting and slowly slide your fingers along the ear to serve as protection for each cut of your blade.

For the eyebrows (area 5 in the picture), you are going to use your thinning shears. The eyebrows should be wider over the inside of the eye and gradually narrow to the point they almost disappear over the outside corner of the eye. Welsh Terrier eyebrows are short. They are shorter than those of the Wire Fox Terrier and Miniature Schnauzer. I think it is especially important to keep the eyebrows short in an older dog with fading vision so the eyebrows don't create shadows and make vision more difficult.

Use thinning shears to blend the hair from the clipped part of the head into the eyebrows. You can also use your thinning shears to shorten the hair at the inside corner of the eyes and underneath the eye (area 5A in the picture). Don't shorten this hair too much and create a hollow. You only want to make sure there is no hair obscuring the eyes.

Use your thinning shears in the area between the eyebrows too. Don't press the blades onto the head. Hold the shears a little away from the skull so that you shorten the hair just enough to differentiate between the two eyebrows. Welsh Terriers do not have a unibrow.

Going forward from the area between the eyes down the narrow strip running to the tip of the nose, you can trim any longish hairs. The

Chapter 7: Grooming Your Welsh Terrier

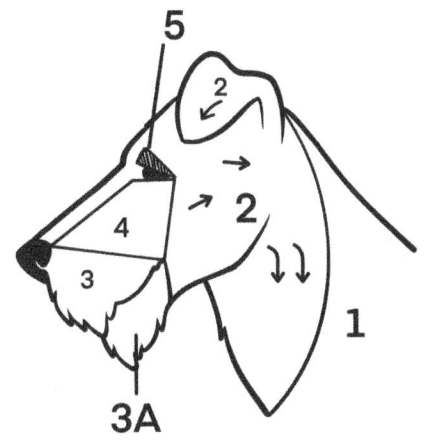

goal is to give the appearance of a straight line running from the forehead to the nose.

With your comb, make a line from the place where the outside top of the nose joins the face and extend it to the top of the outside corner of the lip. (You will see this line in the illustration.) Comb all the hair below this line forward, holding these whiskers with one hand in front of your dog's face. With your other hand, comb and fluff up and out the hair above this line that lies in area 4 of the illustration. Still holding the forward-combed whiskers in one hand, use thinning shears to trim the hair in area 4 to form a surface that is level with the area of the head behind it.

The side of your dog's head should appear as a straight plane from the checks to the end of the whiskers. The top of your dog's head should likewise appear to follow a straight line from the forehead to the nose. Any hair in area 4 that rises above the plane of the forehead to the nose should be trimmed. You are trying to give the impression of a rectangular head with flat, straight planes when viewed from the side or the front. When you have finished trimming area 4 on one side of the face, do the same thing on the other side.

For the whiskers in area 3 on the diagram, comb them forward and use your thinning shears to trim any hairs that stray outside the rectangular plane you are creating. Also, shorten the forward-combed whiskers to a length just past the nose. Underneath the jaw (area 3A on the illustration), you can gradually taper the whiskers into a neat goatee.

You are going to use your thinning shears on the legs and on the lower part of the chest to tidy things up. This is area 6 in the illustration. The front legs should appear to come straight down from the body. In fact, they should be a vertical straight line from the body of the dog down to the bottom of the front legs. Trim these legs into neat little cylinders.

Photo Courtesy of Stephen Long

On the hind legs, use your thinning shears to create a cylindrical appearance from the hock down to the feet. The thinning shears can also tidy up the furnishings from just behind the tuck-up (the place where the leg meets the groin) to the hock. These shears will allow you to blend the hair from the clipped area into the furnishings so it is a gradual lengthening instead of a harsh line between the two areas. Whatever you do, don't give your Welsh Terrier the pantaloon look on its upper thighs. If you look at the dog from the rear, you should see a gradually tapering inverted "U" with nothing suddenly flaring out like a pantaloon.

I usually use a #10 blade on my dog's butt and on the underside of the tail. This keeps the area neat. I also clip under the belly with a #10 blade.

For the feet, you can trim around the feet with your scissors to create tidy feet that look round like a cat's paws when the dog stands. Then, doing one paw at a time, turn the foot upward and scissor the hair between the pads.

When you have finished clipping and scissoring, brush your dog with a bristle brush to remove all the loose hair. I also usually give my dogs a bath to wash off any remaining loose hairs that might be itchy.

The third way to trim your dog is a combination of stripping and clipping. You can clip and scissor the hard parts like the butt and belly and strip easy areas like the jacket.

Bathing

If you regularly brush and comb your Welsh Terrier, it won't need to be bathed very often. You could probably get away with only bathing after the coat is trimmed and anytime your dog gets into something stinky or that won't brush out. If you want to wash your dog more often, a bath every six to eight weeks should be fine. More often might dry out the skin.

If you brush and comb your dog before bathing, less hair will go down the drain, and combing out afterward will be easier. The bath water should be lukewarm because hot water can burn a dog's skin. Use a shampoo made specifically for dogs and rinse several times to make sure you get all the shampoo out of your dog's coat. (I normally dilute a little shampoo with water in a cup prior to bathing and pour this dilution over the dog instead of using straight shampoo.)

First, wet the dog from the back of the neck to the tail and butt, along with the legs and belly. Next, apply shampoo along the neck to the tail and butt and massage it in. Then, apply shampoo to the belly, legs, and feet and massage that in.

You can move on to the face next. Dogs dislike water on their face the most, so I usually leave this for last. You must avoid getting shampoo in your dog's eyes and keep the inside of the ears dry. (Some people advise placing cotton in a dog's ears to keep them dry, but I have never had any luck getting cotton to stay in the ears.) Also, make sure you don't spray water up your dog's nose or mouth because that could cause aspiration pneumonia. If you are worried, you can wash your dog's face using a washcloth to avoid getting water and shampoo in the wrong places.

After you've finished shampooing your Welshie, it's time to rinse, rinse, and rinse again. You want to make sure not to leave any shampoo residue anywhere on your dog that could irritate its skin. Run your hand over your dog's body to make sure you don't feel any soap residue after you have rinsed several times. Make sure to check the elbows, belly, and feet (including between the pads.) If you don't feel any soap residue, then you can stop rinsing.

When you finish bathing your Welshie, don't let it loose because it's likely to race around the house, getting water everywhere. Instead, allow your dog to shake off some excess water, then towel dry it with several large, absorbent bath towels. You want to remove as much water as possible, moving the towels along the jacket in the direction the hair grows. If you rub the jacket in the opposite direction of the hair, you will get a fluffy rather than a flat coat. After towel drying, you can use a hair dryer set on the lowest setting. Hold the dryer away from the coat and keep it moving in the direction the hair grows so you don't burn your dog. When you are done, brush and comb your dog again.

Most dogs don't enjoy being bathed, but they can learn to tolerate it. A bathmat will prevent your dog from slipping and make it feel a little more secure in a bath. I also like to reassure a dog by talking to it while shampooing and rinsing.

Nails

Toenail maintenance is another important part of dog grooming. You should check each week to see if your Welshie's nails need to be trimmed. Long nails don't just look bad; they're more prone to tearing and breaking, can cause foot pain, and can lead to deformed feet and injured tendons.

A Welsh Terrier's nails should end a little above the ground when it's standing or walking. If you can hear the nails clicking on a hard surface as your dog walks, then the nails are too long.

Before you trim, you should know something about your dog's nails. Inside the hard outer shell lies a soft quick with nerves and the blood supply that nourishes the nail. If you cut the quick, it will bleed and cause the dog pain. With light-colored nails, you can see the quick through the hard outer shell, but not with black nails like those of a Welsh Terrier.

The best way to avoid hitting the quick on black toenails is to trim a little at a time and check the surface after each trim. Initially, you will see a white surface inside the nail where you trimmed. Continue removing a bit at a time until you see a gray spot appear at the center of the cut surface. That spot means you are getting close to the quick, and it is time to stop trimming.

If a dog's toenails have grown too long, you'll need to shorten them gradually because the quick will have grown out with the nail. (The quick will recede over time as you shorten the nail.) This can usually be achieved by cutting the nails once a week until they reach the desired length.

You can either use a dog nail clipper or grinder to trim the toenails. With either method, hold your dog firmly but not with a vise-like grip. A Welshie held too tightly will struggle and make nail trimming difficult.

When using a clipper, make a strong, quick cut rather than a slow, gentle one so that you cut the nail cleanly rather than crushing as you cut. Another cause of a crushed, crumbly cut surface is a dull blade. If you think the blade is dull, change it or get a new nail clipper.

With a grinder, pull the hair away from the nail so hair doesn't get caught in it. Also, keep the grinder moving with short strokes to avoid overheating one spot. I like to alternate between nails on one paw at a time when grinding.

Always have styptic powder on hand to stop any bleeding if you accidentally hit the quick. Everyone, even professionals, occasionally hit a quick when trimming dog nails. Just try not to do it too often, or your dog may start to resist having its nails done.

I've never known a dog that loved having its toenails trimmed, but my Welsh Terriers have always calmly accepted the process. With a young puppy or a dog that is fearful of nail trimming, I make one small cut on one nail on the first day, offering treats and praise immediately after. The next day, I repeat this on a different nail. If the dog seems to accept the process, I will do two other nails on the third day. I continue clipping more nails each day so long as the dog accepts it. Eventually, I can clip all the nails on the same day and make as many small cuts as needed on a nail. I use a similar method to accustom dogs to a grinder, except I start by getting the dog used to the sound before I grind even one nail.

If you've never trimmed nails before, ask your vet or breeder to demonstrate. It's not difficult, but if you can't bring yourself to do it, have your vet and/or groomer trim your dog's nails on a regular basis.

Ears

You probably won't need to clean your Welsh Terrier's ears every week, but you should check them once a week. If you notice a mild, unpleasant odor or a little dirt or wax buildup in the ears, it's probably time to clean them. I also like to clean my dog's ears after a bath or a swim.

Every dog is different. Some may only require ear cleaning once every four to eight weeks. Others may need it a little more often. Just remember that excessive cleaning can cause ear problems, so be careful not to overdo it.

You can ask your vet to suggest a good ear cleaner for your dog. (I have always used a veterinarian-recommended commercial ear cleaner on mine.) Be wary of homemade cleaners because some do-it-yourself recipes don't work well or use ingredients that can cause ear problems.

To clean an ear, gently restrain your pet as you lift the ear flap and fill the ear canal with the cleaning solution. Maintaining your hold to prevent the dog from prematurely shaking out the liquid, move your hand to the base of the ear and gently massage where the ear meets the head for about 20 seconds. You will hear the liquid squishing inside the ear as you massage and any gunk inside the ear mixes with the liquid cleaner. Next, allow your dog to shake its head. This should shake the now liquified gunk out of the ear canal.

When your dog finishes shaking, wipe clean the area that you can see inside the ear using a cotton ball or pad. Do one ear completely before moving on to the other. Throughout the process, try to be gentle and reassuring. You can also offer treats as a reward.

Don't swab deep inside your dog's ears because you could damage them. In fact, don't use cotton swabs in a dog's ears. If your pet moves suddenly when you're cleaning the ear with a cotton swab, you could accidentally ram the instrument inside too deeply.

Should your Welshie show any sign of pain when you clean its ears, consult your veterinarian. If your dog's ears are very red, inflamed, painful, itchy, or have an excessive amount of debris, see the veterinarian rather than attempting to clean them yourself. These could be signs that your Welshie has a serious problem, such as an ear infection or ear mites, so a simple home cleaning probably won't help and could be painful. Such conditions don't clear up without proper treatment and tend to get worse and harder to resolve if left untreated.

Your dog's ears should be free of excess hair to allow for good airflow. Keep the hair inside the ear (including the flap) and on the head just in front of the ear trimmed short. From the ear canal, pluck the hairs gently, one or two hairs at a time. I try not to clean the ears on the same day that I pull hair from the ear canal because a cleaning agent may sting the freshly plucked skin.

Eyes

Besides keeping your Welsh Terrier's eyebrows short, you should regularly check its eyes. Healthy dogs' eyes are bright and clear. The whites of the eyes should not appear bloodshot or inflamed and should be as close to pure white as possible.

Signs that your dog may have a serious eye problem include:

- Cloudy or red eyes
- Excessive tearing or discharge
- Increase or change of color/ consistency in tearing or discharge
- Excessive squinting/blinking
- Pawing or rubbing eye

You should contact your veterinarian as soon as possible if your dog exhibits any of these symptoms. Delay in proper medical care for some eye problems can lead to irreversible damage. (We'll look at some specific eye issues in Chapter 8.)

Occasionally, some foreign debris, such as dirt or pollen, may accumulate in a Welsh Terrier's eye. When the eye tries to wash this debris out with tears, a little moisture, clear mucus, or crusty bits may form at the inner corner of the eye. If this is not a common occurrence and the eye looks normal, otherwise, it should be okay to clean this bit of goop yourself. Moisten a gauze pad with lukewarm water and gently run it along the lower eyelid to the inside corner, wiping away from the eye. Be careful not to touch the eye directly, or you might scratch or irritate it. The eye goop should stick to the damp gauze and lift right off. Use a fresh pad for each eye.

You can also flush the eyes with veterinary-recommended eye wash. Ask your vet to suggest a product and show you how to use it. I always flush my dogs' eyes after a bath and after they've been digging in the tunnels at an earth dog trial.

Photo Courtesy of Annie McAnespie

Doggy Dental Care

Just like people, Welsh Terriers can get dental disease, leading to sore gums, root infections, rotting teeth, abscesses, pain, and even systemic health problems. Brushing your dog's teeth can help prevent these problems, so it should be a part of your dog's daily grooming routine.

To brush your Welshie's teeth, you will need toothpaste made for dogs. (Human toothpaste has ingredients that are toxic to dogs.) A dog toothbrush or a fingertip toothbrush for dogs is also necessary. And don't forget to always give plenty of praise and treats during a toothbrushing session.

If your Welsh Terrier is not used to having its teeth brushed, introduce the process slowly. Start by putting a dab of dog toothpaste on your finger and letting the dog sniff and lick it. Next, use your finger to rub toothpaste on your Welshie's front teeth. Do this for a few days, then try rubbing it on all the teeth.

When your dog is comfortable with this, you can put a dab of toothpaste on the toothbrush and let your Welshie lick it off. Then you can start brushing the front teeth with the brush. As your dog becomes more comfortable with the brush, you can slowly include more teeth. Eventually, your Welshie will calmly allow you to brush all its teeth.

I brush only the outer surface of a dog's teeth near the gum line because the tongue helps keep the inner tooth surfaces clean. Since plaque and tartar seem to build up more on the back teeth, try to give a little extra attention to those teeth. (You'll find more dental health information in Chapter 8.)

Final Thoughts on Grooming

> *Grooming helps develop a bond between owner and dog while giving the opportunity to check toes, skin, and inside the ears for anything untoward. Five or 10 minutes a day is plenty for a pet, and the dog should enjoy the attention.*
>
> **PAUL SPRAGG**
> *Westpenn*

If, for some reason, your Welsh Terrier can't be groomed regularly, you should at least keep the hair trimmed short inside the ears and around the anus and clip or grind the toenails as needed. This should not be the norm, but if you are going through a hectic time, your Welshie can get by temporarily with this minimal attention to grooming.

CHAPTER 8

Health Care

When you acquire a Welsh Terrier, you are making a commitment to ensure its lifelong happiness and health. This includes managing its health care, diet, exercise, and grooming.

An important part of this responsibility is an annual (or biannual) veterinary visit with a thorough physical exam. These preventive checkups include blood, fecal, and urine tests, parasite preventatives, vaccinations, and, sometimes, dental care.

Your veterinarian should see your new terrier soon after its arrival in your home. The initial visit (along with any past health records you provide) will help form a baseline of your dog's health condition. In the future, this baseline may help your veterinarian discover health issues when they first appear.

Vaccinations

Vaccines help your Welsh Terrier's immune system fight off potentially fatal disease-causing organisms. Your veterinarian will develop a schedule of inoculations based on the dog's age, vaccination history, lifestyle, and location.

Vaccines recommended for all dogs are called core vaccines. A Welsh Terrier should begin these vaccinations when it is around six to eight weeks old. A puppy receives core combination vaccinations for distemper, adenovirus type 2, and parvovirus (parainfluenza may also be included). It is impossible to predict when a young dog's immune system will respond fully to vaccination and provide complete protection. So, a puppy must receive a scheduled series of shots from six to sixteen weeks of age. Until it has completed this shot series, your puppy needs to

Chapter 8: Health Care

Photo Courtesy of Viktoria Ginzery

be shielded from potential exposure to these viruses. Rabies is another core vaccination. A Welsh Terrier should receive its first rabies shot at around 16 weeks.

As an adult, a Welshie will need booster shots of these core vaccines. When a dog must receive its rabies booster is usually dictated by law throughout the United States. You can discuss with your veterinarian when your adult Welsh Terrier needs boosters for other vaccines. Your veterinarian can use a blood test to check the vaccine titers of your dog. If a vaccine titer is found to be sufficient, then your pet still has enough immunity that it may not yet need a booster shot.

Non-core vaccines are typically only given on an as-needed basis. Whether your dog needs these vaccinations will depend on the prevalence of a disease in the area you live and your dog's potential for exposure. Lyme disease, canine influenza, leptospirosis, and Bordetella vaccines are some non-core examples. Your veterinarian can advise you on non-core vaccinations for your Welshie. (If you plan to travel with your dog, it's a good idea to ask your vet if your pet will need additional shots.)

Internal and External Parasites

As your Welshie explores the world, investigating stinky smells and running through vegetation, it will inevitably encounter both external and internal parasites. In fact, most dogs will get intestinal worms as puppies, either from their mother or their environment. A breeder should provide information about fecal tests performed and any worm treatments given to your puppy. It is important to take this information along with a fecal sample when you visit the veterinarian for the first time.

Four types of intestinal worms are common in dogs: tapeworms, roundworms, hookworms, and whipworms. Segments of tapeworms can sometimes be seen in the dog's poop. (They look like tiny rice grains.) The other three worms always require a microscopic examination of a fecal sample to find.

If your veterinarian diagnoses worms in your dog, he will advise the best treatment for the type of worm. Sometimes it will require a series of treatments because the first treatment may only kill the adult worms but not the worm eggs. Future treatment will be timed to kill the worms that hatch from those eggs.

Signs your dog may have intestinal worms include:

- Diarrhea
- Blood or mucus in the stool
- Scooting and chewing its behind
- Vomiting
- Lethargy
- Dull, dry coat
- Potbelly
- Unexplained weight loss

Dogs get intestinal worms from ingesting the spores or eggs in contaminated water, soil, food, feces, or (in the case of tapeworms) fleas. So, if your Welsh Terrier has tapeworms, you will want to make sure both the dog and the environment are free of fleas in addition to deworming your pet. It is always best to keep your dog's environment as clean as possible and provide plenty of safe chew toys.

Intestinal worms can be a serious health issue for young puppies and lead to poor growth. Initially, a healthy adult Welsh Terrier may not exhibit symptoms from a new worm infestation, but over time, an untreated infestation will eventually cause problems. Dogs cannot get rid of a worm infestation without treatment.

Heartworm is a serious disease caused by the worm Dirofilaria immitis that lives, grows, and multiplies inside your dog's heart. It is spread by mosquito bites. Affected canines become seriously ill and can die. Treatment is very expensive, takes a long time, and can cause serious side effects. It is much better to give your Welsh Terrier medication to prevent heartworms. Your vet will perform a blood test to check for heartworms in your Welshie before prescribing a preventative. Testing is necessary because the preventive medication can be harmful to a dog already infected with heartworm. Some heartworm preventatives also help prevent intestinal worm infestations.

External parasites live on the outside of a Welsh Terrier and can be found hiding in the coat. The most common ones are fleas and ticks. Ear mites, Cheyletiella mites, scabies (Sarcoptic mange), Demodex, and lice are found less frequently. (Lice are species-specific, so humans aren't usually bitten by dog lice, unlike fleas, which don't discriminate between dogs and humans.)

> **HEALTH ALERT**
> **Identifying Lens Luxation**
>
> Welsh Terriers are a hardy breed with few health concerns. Despite their healthy dispositions, Welsh Terriers may be more likely than other dogs to develop an ocular condition called lens luxation. This condition occurs when the lens inside the eye becomes dislocated. Symptoms of lens luxation include:
> - Increased tears or blinking
> - Sudden change in size or shape of the pupil
> - Vision loss
> - Redness or cloudiness of the eye
>
> Only a veterinarian can diagnose lens luxation. However, early detection of lens luxation can improve your dog's prognosis, so don't hesitate to contact your veterinarian at the first signs of an ocular issue.

You want to watch for and regularly check your dog for signs of external parasites, which include:

- Excessive scratching
- Black debris or brown discharge in ears
- Tiny black flecks of dried flea blood
- Hair loss
- Skin rash
- Scabs

Fortunately, a variety of flea and tick preventatives are also effective against lice and mites. Additionally, if you walk your Welsh Terrier in areas with lots of vegetation, running a sticky lint roller over the dog's entire body soon after an excursion may help remove ticks before they attach to your terrier. You can also discuss the Lyme vaccine with your veterinarian if the area where you live has a high rate of Lyme disease.

If your dog is bitten by a tick or infested with any external parasites, your veterinarian will be able to determine the best course of treatment. The other pets in a household, as well as bedding, furniture, linen, and carpets, may also need to be treated.

How to Help Your Welsh Terrier Live Longer

> *Feeding your Welshie a premium food or feeding raw is more expensive but will save you a great deal on veterinary expenses in the long run. Source all foods and treats and read the labels carefully, just as you would do for yourself.*
>
> **ELIZABETH BERRY**
> *Airedale and Welsh Terrier Rescue*

Chapter 8: Health Care

You love your Welsh Terrier and want to keep it healthy. In addition to regular veterinary checkups, vaccination, and parasite control, some other things you can do to help your dog live longer include:

- Feed your dog a nutritious and balanced diet.
- Maintain your terrier at a healthy weight. Obesity is hard on a Welshie's joints, makes it more likely to develop an illness, and shortens its life span.
- Exercise your dog, but don't overdo it. Exercise builds muscle to support your pet's joints. Know your dog's limits. A very young dog or a senior dog may want to keep racing around even after it's exhausted or overheated. You must make sure your dog takes a break when it needs one.
- I believe that exercising the brain helps keep a Welsh Terrier cognitively healthy. Even an old dog can enjoy practicing easy tricks or playing with interactive dog puzzles.
- Pay attention to changes in your dog. Notice health issues before they become serious, if possible. Modify your dog's routine and diet as senior limitations necessitate.
- Brushing a terrier's teeth, dental chews, and dental rinses can help prevent gingivitis. Plaque and tartar buildup can cause serious health issues in dogs, just like in humans. If a dog has bad breath, seems to have trouble eating, or has plaque buildup on its teeth, your Welshie may need teeth cleaning by the veterinarian. Many dogs require occasional dental cleanings to maintain a healthy mouth.
- Regular grooming keeps your Welshie's coat and nails in shape and helps you notice any new lumps and bumps that pop up on its body.
- Give your dog your attention and affection. Welsh Terriers are very sociable dogs, and positive attention and affection from you help keep endorphins and oxytocin levels up.
- Spay/neuter your pet. We tend to think of sterilization as helping to fight pet overpopulation, but it also has some health benefits for your terrier. Spaying a female dog has been shown to reduce the risk of mammary cancer, especially if done before her first heat cycle. It can also prevent a bitch from developing a uterine infection (pyometra). Testicular tumors are a common occurrence in older intact

males but do occasionally occur in younger dogs. These tumors can produce estrogen, cause discomfort, and are sometimes malignant. Castration is the primary treatment as well as a preventative. On the other hand, while gonadectomy may reduce male urine marking and roaming in search of bitches in heat, research shows that spaying or neutering doesn't prevent or solve most behavioral issues in dogs. Those require training.

Welsh Terrier Health Problems

> *Some dogs are deficient in Vitamin D, which can cause a variety of health problems. It is a good idea to discuss with your vet whether your dog is showing any signs of this deficiency and if a blood test for Vitamin D should be given. This condition is easily treated, and could be especially important for dogs that are over five years of age.*
>
> **JUDITH FORD ANSPACH**
> *Abbeyrose Welsh Terriers*

The Welsh Terrier tends to be a robust breed. However, there are a few health problems that sometimes occur in these dogs.

One issue is eye problems. For many years, breeders lived in fear that glaucoma would pop up in the Welsh Terriers they were breeding. It was suspected to be a genetic problem, but no one was sure of the mode of inheritance. Also, there was no way to test for animals at risk of developing glaucoma.

Then, after many breeders and pet owners donated DNA samples from affected breeds, scientists developed a DNA test for Primary Lens Luxation (PLL). This is a painful condition where the lens is dislocated from its normal position in the eye, causing inflammation and glaucoma.

Chapter 8: Health Care

Photo Courtesy of Cindy Duber

Photo Courtesy of Tina Caldwell

It was discovered that some Welsh Terriers carried the gene for this eye disorder.

Dogs with just one copy of the PLL gene are considered carriers and generally do not go on to develop lens luxation. Dogs with two copies of the gene are considered affected and are likely to develop lens luxation eventually. Dogs that do not have a copy of this gene are considered clear.

Hopefully, the breeder of your Welsh Terrier tested its parents for PLL before breeding. (Breeding two carriers to each other or a carrier to an affected dog is not considered good breeding practice.) If your breeder did not test the parents for lens luxation, you can discuss this issue with your veterinarian. I would strongly urge testing your Welshie for the gene if you don't know the status of its parents. If your dog tests clear or turns out just to be a carrier, you don't have to worry about it developing the genetic form of lens luxation. If it tests affected for lens luxation, you should probably consult a veterinary ophthalmologist.

Welsh Terriers sometimes develop cataracts. That is an additional reason to have a dog checked out by a veterinary ophthalmologist. It is possible to remove canine cataracts and replace the lens with an artificial one.

If your terrier's eyes are bloodshot and seem to be causing pain or discomfort (the dog may be rubbing its eyes), regardless of its genetics, this is also a sign that it needs to be seen by an ophthalmologist. Don't delay seeking a specialist eye examination for your Welshie. Canine eyes are very complicated, and general practitioner veterinarians don't usually have the specialized equipment to diagnose canine eye problems thoroughly. Some eye conditions can rapidly lead to blindness if left untreated.

Hypothyroidism is another health issue that Welsh Terriers occasionally develop. This happens when the thyroid gland in a canine does not secrete enough thyroid hormones. Symptoms can include lethargy, weight gain, a dull coat with excessive shedding, hair loss, skin infections, and ear infections.

Your veterinarian will run thyroid tests and consider your Welsh Terrier's complete medical history before diagnosing hypothyroidism. (Some other illnesses and medications can affect thyroid levels without a dog having hypothyroidism.) If your dog is diagnosed with this problem, it can be successfully treated but not cured. Thyroid replacement therapy is the treatment, and once started, a dog will need to have its thyroid levels checked periodically for the rest of its life. With treatment, the prognosis for a dog with hypothyroidism is good.

Another health problem that sometimes occurs in Welsh Terriers is congenital megaesophagus (ME). In this disease, the esophageal muscles lack tone and motility, and the esophagus stretches. Food does not reach the stomach and is instead effortlessly regurgitated. There is no heaving to vomit. The food just slides back out of the dog's mouth. This problem is usually recognizable as soon as the puppy is weaned, if not before.

Dogs with congenital ME generally have a poor prognosis. They are prone to aspiration pneumonia from breathing in the food as it is being regurgitated and tend not to thrive due to a lack of nourishment. A breeder can usually spot congenital ME before a puppy is sold. (ME in adult dogs can also be caused by other diseases and toxins. This is called Acquired Megaesophagus.)

Some owners of ME-affected Welsh Terriers have been able to manage the disease and provide their dogs with quality of life for a number of years. Milder cases may be helped by feeding frequent small meals of soft food from a raised dish so that gravity can assist the esophagus.

A great resource for anyone with an affected dog is the nonprofit Upright Canine Brigade at caninemegaesophagusinfo.com. Their website helps educate people about this problem and provides techniques for managing it, as well as providing news about the latest research. It even lists member-recommended veterinarians who are experienced in treating ME.

Epilepsy is another problem that sometimes affects Welsh Terriers. According to the Canine Epilepsy Network, research shows that up to four percent of all dogs (mixed breed and purebred) are affected by this disease.

Epilepsy is a neurological illness that causes electrical storms in the brain resulting in repeated seizures. Some symptoms of a seizure include collapsing, small twitches, loss of bowel or bladder control, stiffening, and body convulsions. The Canine Epilepsy Network website (http://www.canine-epilepsy.net/) provides a good description of the various types of seizures.

There are many things besides epilepsy that can cause seizures in dogs, including ingested toxins, high or low blood sugar, brain cancer, liver disease, and kidney disease. A disease called paroxysmal dyskinesia, which has been diagnosed in a few Welsh Terriers, causes episodes of involuntary muscle activity that can be mistakenly diagnosed as epilepsy.

Some things you should do or not do if your dog is having a seizure include:

- Make sure your dog is in a safe, open space where it can't injure itself.
- Don't put your hand in its mouth, as it may clamp down during a seizure.
- Don't try to give oral medication because your terrier could choke on it.
- Time the seizure. Most are very brief, but if it lasts more than five minutes or has occurred several times in one day, seek emergency veterinary care immediately.
- Record a video of the episode if possible. (An accurate description or recording of a seizure can help your veterinarian distinguish epilepsy from paroxysmal dyskinesia.)
- Talk gently to your pet to reassure it during the event.
- Call your vet or emergency vet as soon as possible after the seizure ends. If poisoning is suspected, call a pet poison control helpline and/or rush your dog to a veterinarian. (You will find information on pet poison control helplines listed in resources at the back of this book.)

Your vet will want to do a physical exam and some lab work to determine the cause of a seizure. If your terrier is diagnosed with epilepsy, appropriate medication may make it possible for your dog to have a good quality of life.

Chapter 8: Health Care

Just like humans, Welsh Terriers sometimes have allergies. The most common culprits are food, flea, and environmental/seasonal allergies. If you suspect your pet has allergies, consult your veterinarian. (You may be referred to a veterinary dermatologist for environmental hypersensitivities.) The first step in diagnosing this issue is usually ruling out other problems. Allergies cannot be cured but can be treated once correctly diagnosed.

Photo Courtesy of Mary Duafala

If your Welsh Terrier is diagnosed with a medical problem, you should notify its breeder. He/she may have experience and valuable advice on the issue. Plus, responsible breeders want to know about health problems in their dogs because that knowledge helps keep the gene pool healthy. (Buying from a breeder who tracks health issues in order to maintain sound breeding stock is your best insurance for getting a healthy dog.)

Is It an Emergency?

Unfortunately, pet health emergencies happen. When it happens during your veterinarian's regular hours, you can call and ask whether you should bring your dog in. However, sometimes, it's hard to know if your Welsh Terrier needs to rush to the emergency veterinarian in the middle of the night.

Reasons an emergency veterinary visit is necessary include the following:

- Seizures
- Difficulty breathing

- Excessive bleeding
- Pale or grayish gums
  - You can test capillary refill in a dog's gums by pressing on them. After you press on the gum and remove your finger, the gum color should be temporarily pale but return to a healthy pink almost immediately. If the color doesn't return quickly, your pet may have a problem with circulation.
- Loss of consciousness
- Staggering or unable to stand
- Paralysis
- Vomiting and/or diarrhea that lasts more than 24 hours or is excessive
- Large quantity of blood in vomit, feces, or urine
- Extreme pain or restlessness
- Poison ingestion
  - Your dog's life may depend on how quickly it receives veterinary attention after ingesting poison.
- Extreme allergic reaction affecting breathing
- Trauma such as being hit by a car or falling from a balcony
- Eye injury or sudden blindness
- Heatstroke
- Inability to bear weight on a limb
- Inability to urinate
- Not eating or drinking for a day or more

This is only a partial list. If a situation arises and you are not sure if your Welsh Terrier needs the emergency veterinarian, sometimes it is just better to go with your gut because you know your dog best.

First Aid

Two things every Welsh Terrier owner should have are a canine first aid manual and a canine first aid kit. A good first aid book will give detailed instructions for various pet emergencies and include things like CPR and the Heimlich maneuver for pets. You can easily find these on Amazon.

One item that should be in your pet's first aid kit is a thermometer. A dog's temperature is taken rectally. Put a little Vaseline on the end of the thermometer and then slowly insert it about one inch into your dog's anus. The temperature should register after about 60 seconds. After you remove the thermometer, remember to clean it. The normal temperature for a dog ranges between 100.5 to 102.5 degrees Fahrenheit.

Another thing you should always have on hand for pet emergencies is a muzzle. I've never had to use a muzzle on one of my own dogs, but I did supply one for a dog that broke its leg near my house. That poor dog was in agony, and its owner was unable to move it because it was biting in pain. After the muzzle was placed on the dog, I drove it and the owner to the vet, where the dog had surgery to repair its leg.

Pet Insurance

Veterinary care for a dog is very expensive, and a pet insurance policy may make it more affordable. These plans reimburse you for a certain amount of your veterinary bill. First, you pay the vet, and then you send the insurance company a copy of the paid vet bill. A few weeks later, you get a check from your pet insurance company for a portion of that veterinary bill.

There are different types of pet insurance plans to choose from, including Wellness, Accident Only, and Accident and Illness. They pretty much are what they sound like. Wellness policies cover preventive veterinary care like vaccinations and regular checkups. Accident Only policies cover only accidents, and Accident and Illness policies cover accidents and illnesses. You may also be able to create a customized plan for your Welsh Terrier.

Talk to your vet about whether he/she thinks pet insurance policies help clients and which insurance companies seem the best. Also, talk to your breeder and dog-owning friends to find out what they think of pet health insurance.

CHAPTER 9

Building Confidence and Making Friends— Human & Canine

> *I recommend starting early—immediately after vaccination, if possible. Take your Welsh Terrier to show training, obedience classes, or just general socialization classes. Puppies need to mix with their own kind and be praised when they're doing well and gently chastised when they're not. Using the correct tone of voice is essential—keep it happy, cheerful, and lighthearted for giving praise, and avoid eye contact while using a stern or serious tone for poor behavior.*
>
> **PAUL SPRAGG**
> *Westpenn*

An adult Welsh Terrier should be a friendly, outgoing, and curious dog that is happy to make new friends with people and dogs it meets. This attitude does not magically occur. A Welshie's behavioral tendencies must be nurtured through proper socialization and training, particularly at a young age.

Chapter 9: Building Confidence and Making Friends—Human & Canine

Photo Courtesy of Steve Ambrosio

Why Early Socialization Is Important

A puppy's brain is like a sponge during the first three to four months of its life, eagerly soaking up new experiences and storing them for future reference. You help your puppy develop into a well-adjusted, friendly adult by providing a variety of positive exposures to people of all ages, dogs, sights, sounds, smells, objects, and environments during this period. Between eight to ten weeks of age, a puppy goes through its first fear period, and it's important to go slow with new experiences and not overwhelm the youngster during this brief phase. (See Chapter 2 for more information on fear periods and how to deal with them.)

The time spent socializing a puppy before the age of four months pays off when it matures into an outgoing, confident adult Welsh Terrier. This is a dog whose foundation of positive experiences gives it confidence even after four months of age when it is natural to become more cautious of new things. A Welshie that did not have this wealth of positive exposures during its first four months can still be socialized, but it will take much more time and effort than it would have at a younger age.

(After the age of four months, it is more a process of desensitization than socialization.)

Even after the prime age has passed, I believe it's a good idea to keep socializing a dog. Continued exposure to positive novel experiences may prevent a Welshie from developing some behavioral issues. However, if you make your dog a recluse, the memories of socialization may fade, and it may become leery of new things.

Tips for Socializing Your Puppy

> *Young puppies must be kept away from areas where unvaccinated dogs have been, but at the same time exposed to as many other dogs as possible. A well-run puppy class can provide a safe environment to interact with other puppies, as well as new people, sights, sounds, and surfaces. Puppies need to be protected from any dog that truly frightens them, but learning to chase, wrestle, and roll with other pups can build confidence.*
>
> **LUCY BAILEY**
> *WYSIWYG Welsh Terriers*

Socialization is a process that helps a Welsh Terrier acclimate to unfamiliar sights, sounds, objects, people, and other animals. It starts with the breeder and continues when the dog moves to your home.

You need to manage the process carefully to ensure that experiences are positive; otherwise, your Welshie may learn to dislike or fear certain things. Punishment such as yelling and hitting should NEVER be part of a dog's socialization and training.

Chapter 9: Building Confidence and Making Friends—Human & Canine

At home, be creative in finding things to introduce to your new dog:

- Place a tarp on the floor and encourage the Welshie to explore it.
- A ladder lying on the floor can be another item to explore. Encourage your terrier to approach and smell the ladder and then step over its rungs.
- Show your puppy the vacuum cleaner when it is turned off. Later, turn on the vacuum and let it hear the motor while enjoying treats or playing with a toy.
- Introduce your Welshie to an umbrella (closed and open).

Photo Courtesy of Martha Sagers

If your terrier exhibits distress when exposed to something new, move it further away from the situation until it is relaxed enough to enjoy a treat or toy. (Toys and treats can be useful distractions for a fearful puppy.) Over time, your Welshie should be able to move closer to whatever worries it without becoming uncomfortable.

Try to remember the following when socializing a young Welsh Terrier:

- Be patient.
- Start small, and don't rush the process.
- Stay positive. Use praise, treats, and toys to make these experiences fun for your dog.
- Do not force interactions. Allow your Welshie to move away from a situation if it wants to, and don't hold the leash too tightly. Your dog should not feel trapped or cornered.
- Don't reward fear; ignore it.
- If your dog is less than 16 weeks old, sign it up for a well-run puppy class. (See Chapter 5 for more information on puppy classes.)

You should avoid taking a puppy that is not fully vaccinated to places unvaccinated dogs might frequent. That includes dog parks, public parks, and beaches.

Some things you can do with a puppy before it's completely vaccinated:

- Visit stores that allow dogs and carry your puppy around the store.
- Visit friends that either don't have dogs or whose dogs are puppy friendly and fully vaccinated.
- Once your puppy is comfortable with multiple people visiting, invite a group of friends over to watch TV.
- Host a playdate for puppies that attend your puppy class.

Teaching Your Dog How to Greet People

You want your Welsh Terrier to meet a wide variety of adults and children during socialization. That includes people of different genders, sizes, ages, and even ethnicities. Manage these interactions and explain to people how to interact with your puppy as it learns good manners. Ask that everyone use a calm, pleasant voice with your Welshie and not engage in rough play that will excite your pet. Also, remember a young puppy tires quickly, so keep introductions short or allow your puppy a brief nap away from the excitement.

To teach your dog to greet people calmly, I recommend you teach it to sit on command. This is a simple exercise, even for young puppies. I usually begin with the lure technique to teach my Welshies to sit. (See Chapter 11 for detailed instructions.)

I also recommend ignoring unwanted behavior and lavishly rewarding good behavior. I've taught whole litters to sit for attention by ignoring them until one of them sat and then immediately rewarding that puppy. Soon, all the Welshies in the litter were competing for who could sit first to get attention. Whatever method you choose, practice it often.

Before your friends and family come over to visit, tell them it will take you a few minutes to answer the door when they ring the doorbell or knock. I also suggest leaving either a bag of treats or a toy hanging on the door for them to use as a reward for your puppy upon entering your home.

Chapter 9: Building Confidence and Making Friends—Human & Canine

When the doorbell rings, put a leash on your Welsh Terrier and have it sit. Once it sits, give a reward before opening the door. After entering, your guest should ask your puppy to sit and reward the behavior with either a treat or a toy. If you repeat this exercise every time someone visits, your Welshie will learn to find you so it can sit for a reward when the doorbell rings.

If your puppy is too excited and doesn't sit for the guest, ignore it until it sits. Then your visitor can immediately reward your pet with praise, treats, and attention.

Should your Welshie become too excited during a visit, you can place it in a crate with a chew toy until it calms down. Then, try again to get your puppy to behave calmly with your guest.

As long as your puppy remains calm and obedient, your guest can reward that behavior with treats and gentle petting. It's important that a young Welsh Terrier get used to being handled by different people.

In public, ask strangers not to pet your dog until it is sitting. Explain that you are training it to greet people politely. If someone doesn't listen and tries to pet your Welshie when it isn't sitting or, worse, is trying to jump, politely remove your dog from the situation. You don't have to let anyone encourage your dog to misbehave.

Introducing Your Welsh Terrier to Other People's Dogs

Socializing with other dogs is important, but until a Welshie is fully vaccinated, make sure that all the dogs it meets are vaccinated and not exposed to unvaccinated dogs. (Dogs that regularly visit dog parks should be avoided until a youngster is completely vaccinated.) They should also be friendly with puppies.

You can invite friends with dogs to come to your home individually or visit them with your puppy. You should watch out that an older, larger dog is not so energetic that your little puppy is overwhelmed or vice versa. If their play gets too wild, it is probably time for a quiet break for your Welshie.

Photo Courtesy of Katie Cane

For the initial introduction, both dogs should be on leashes in a large enclosed setting. The dogs should see each other from a short distance and, if both appear sociable, approach on loose leads. If they seem friendly, their leashes can be dropped temporarily. (The dragging leashes allow for quick restraint if things get out of hand.) Leashes and collars can be removed after a few moments when all is going well so that play can proceed. (Collars are a choking hazard if one dog's teeth become stuck on another dog's collar.)

I especially like my puppies to interact with well-mannered adult dogs that will let a youngster know when it gets out of line. These older nanny dogs teach a puppy how to behave with other canines. The older dog should be able to tell a puppy to mind its manners with a quick reprimand (sometimes just a warning snarl) and then continue playing with it. The older dog should not be overly aggressive or a bully with the puppy. At the same time, don't let your puppy become a hyperactive terror for the other canine.

A puppy class offers a young Welshie the chance to socialize with a variety of puppies of similar age. Just be watchful that your Welsh Terrier is not bullied or bullying when playing with the other puppies. A good puppy class instructor will watch out for this behavior, and you should too.

When your Welshie is fully vaccinated, it's time to teach that it isn't allowed to meet every dog and how to meet strange dogs politely. First, you must practice walking on a leash at home without distractions and then gradually add distractions. You want to teach your terrier to focus on you using treats or a toy.

I teach my young dogs a trick to help them focus on me instead of distractions on walks. I begin teaching this trick while standing still with the dog on a leash beside me and facing forward. Holding a treat in the hand that is next to the terrier, I have it follow that hand in a small circle. First, moving away from me and then finishing beside me, facing forward. When

Chapter 9: Building Confidence and Making Friends—Human & Canine

the dog finishes the circle and is beside me again, I give it the treat. I use a one-word command every time a dog follows the treat to circle beside me. My Welshies learn to do this on both my right and left sides.

As your dog understands the trick, you can do it while walking. Then slowly add in distractions. Your Welshie should learn to focus on you and not the distraction while performing this trick. (See Chapter 10 for more about practicing with distractions.) Your terrier will eventually be able to do this trick multiple times in a row as you walk by a barking dog and stay focused on you.

When I am walking a youngster and see another dog, I always place my terrier so that my body is between it and the other dog. I want to signal to my Welshie that I control the situation. Sometimes we walk past the other dog without stopping. Other times, if the owner says their dog is friendly, I may let the dogs meet for just a moment. If my Welshie or the other dog becomes overexcited or rude, I immediately call (in a cheerful tone) my terrier away and continue our walk. It is not a good idea to yell at or scold your dog when it is interacting with another canine, as the Welshie may associate your negativity with the other dog.

I keep these meetings short. It's a simple meet and greet, not a playdate.

Welsh Terriers and Small Children

> *Welsh Terriers are not a good match for homes with babies or small children. Things that move fast and make noise, like young children, tend to set off their prey drive. They will chase, nip at ankles, grab shoes, and bite hands. These are behaviors that are natural to dogs but dangerous to babies or toddlers. But, by elementary school age, children should be able to understand and follow rules like leaving the dog alone while it is eating and always keeping gates and doors shut.*
>
> **JUDITH FORD ANSPACH**
> *Abbeyrose Welsh Terriers*

Photo Courtesy of Diane Amendola

Puppies should be socialized with children so they learn to behave around them as well as like them. These interactions always require supervision. However, young children sometimes poke and pull things even when supervised, so prepare the terrier to accept a little uncomfortable handling.

To desensitize your Welshie to slightly rougher little hands, gently poke its body or pull its ears, tail, or hair. Then, immediately give it a high-value treat. Start gently, and do it once a day in the beginning. As the dog learns to accept this behavior, you can gradually increase the light pokes and pulls to several times in a row and offer a fabulous reward afterward. Don't be so rough that your dog becomes upset. The goal is to teach your dog to expect a reward after uncomfortable handling rather than becoming upset.

HISTORICAL FACT

A Welshie Coat of Arms

Clement Attlee, 1st Earl Attlee and prime minister of the United Kingdom from 1945 to 1951, had a Welsh Terrier named Ting. The dog was so beloved by Attlee that the earl had his canine companion commemorated in the Earl Attlee's coat-of-arms.

If you don't have children, invite friends and family with children to visit. Even if you have children, your Welshie should meet other children because you want them to accept your children's friends in the future.

Invite individual children at first. When your Welsh Terrier is comfortable with one child, gradually increase the number of children visiting. Make sure the kids know how to behave with your dog. You don't want them to unwittingly scare/hurt your pet or encourage misbehavior. For instance, a child should never hug your Welsh Terrier because it may mistake this human affection for aggression. Also, the puppy should have space to move away from children if it wants.

Have your Welshie sit for a child to greet and pet. I like to reward my puppies with a treat every time they sit when interacting with a child. If either the dog or child becomes overexcited, it's time to end the interaction calmly.

Once a Welsh Terrier is fully vaccinated, you can allow young strangers you encounter on walks to meet your dog. Always tell children how to behave with your dog before they greet it, and don't allow anyone to pet your dog without your permission. Give your pup a treat when it sits calmly to meet a strange child, and also give treats as the child gently pets it. Keep these introductions short, and then calmly continue your walk.

Being a Good Neighbor

Let your neighbors know about your new Welsh Terrier, and when it's ready, introduce them. Don't be afraid to tell your neighbor how to interact with your pet. They will probably appreciate that you are being responsible and teaching your dog good manners. Provide treats for them to reward your dog's good behavior. Also, make sure your neighbors know they can communicate with you if they ever have an issue with your dog.

These are some of the ways a Welsh Terrier owner can be a good neighbor:

- Training your dog. A well-behaved dog makes the best neighbor.
- Cleaning up after your dog in your yard and on walks.
- Leaving your dog indoors when you are not home.
- Supervising your dog outdoors and managing barking. If your dog is barking, bring it indoors or provide a distraction. Don't allow your dog to fence-fight with a neighbor's dog.
- Staying off private property when walking your Welshie unless you have permission.
- Keeping your dog secured on a leash or inside a fence outdoors.

Photo Courtesy of Jill See

Peter See and GCH Andover See-z The Moment

There are always people who insist it is safe for their dog to run loose in their community because the roads have very little traffic. Unfortunately, it only takes one car to kill a dog. But that is not the only problem with loose dogs. They can damage other people's property, harass animals, and frighten people who are afraid of dogs. I once witnessed a friendly little poodle chasing its next-door neighbors. The dog thought it was playing, but the people were terrified because they were afraid of dogs.

Chapter 9: Building Confidence and Making Friends—Human & Canine

Photo Courtesy of Bonnie Humphries

Dog Laws

States and municipalities usually have various laws affecting dogs. Understanding and abiding by these regulations can help you avoid problems with your neighbors. Dog laws pertaining to licensing, leashing, vaccinating, cleaning up poop, barking, and other things are in place to protect society, but they can also benefit your Welsh Terrier. For instance, when licensing your pet, you provide identifying information and are given id tags for it to wear. This makes it easier to contact you if your dog ever gets lost.

CHAPTER 10

Training

> *Formal training classes should be started as soon as the dog's vaccination schedule allows, but the owner needs to realize that this is not a 'one class and done' situation—training and reenforcing training should be something that continues throughout the dog's lifetime. Training needs to be positive and fun for the dog. It should include high-value treats that it only receives as rewards during training, and 'jackpots' of more than the usual number of treats should be given when the dog offers a better than usual response.*
>
> **JUDITH FORD ANSPACH**
> *Abbeyrose Welsh Terriers*

Welsh Terriers were originally bred to be independent problem solvers. They are smart, energetic, easily bored, and respond well to positive reinforcement. Reward-based training works best with a Welshie.

Unfortunately, there are some trainers who believe terriers are hard to train. It's true that without proper training and boundaries, a terrier's prey drive, energy, and tenacity can lead it into trouble. Fighting against those traits makes training a Welshie difficult. However, if you know how to use prey drive and harness that energy and tenacity, training any terrier can be fun and easy.

Chapter 10: Training

*Photo Courtesy of
Annie McAnespie*

Photo Courtesy of C & H Saito

> As someone with nearly fifty years of experience as a professional animal trainer, I can unequivocally state that terriers are not only trainable but that training them should be easy and pleasurable for both trainer and trainee. It seems that the reputation they have for being "difficult, stubborn, independent," or whatever description the trainer without experience chooses to give them, comes from two distinct places. The first is from trainers trying to fit them into a mold they will not fit, rather than learning better and easier training techniques, and the second from owners who, rather than admit their own shortcomings when they fail, chalk up their dogs' lack of training to the breed. I have trained well over a hundred terriers, my own and clients', for everything from film and television to the highest levels of competition agility, as well as in obedience and for simple companionship. They are always my favorite dogs to work with on set because they are the easiest.

That said, it can be tricky to find a trainer who is versed in terrier training. Knowing what to look for can help you avoid pitfalls and make the entire experience more enjoyable. While it's not imperative to find a trainer with terrier experience, you want a trainer who encourages the dogs in their class to have fun and stresses a training environment in which the dogs *are set up for success. A good trainer will work with whatever motivates the dog—treats, toys, and praise—and will also work to motivate the handler. If you can watch a class to see the trainer at work, look for one in which the students are having fun. A trainer who can motivate human students is usually pretty good at motivating canine students as well.*

While it is a huge red flag to me when I hear a trainer say things like, "Well, what do you expect from a terrier?" or other excuses rather than helping with training solutions when needed, I also look for a trainer who respects that terriers have specific skills outside of companion sports. Just as many of the top Border Collies in agility enjoy dabbling in herding, terriers training in agility can also benefit from using their natural instincts in Earthdog during their free time. While some people superstitiously believe that letting dogs participate in Earthdog can make them harder to train, there is no factual basis for this, and in my experience, any dog of any breed allowed to fulfill its natural instincts can only benefit from such pursuits. Among my current terrier students is the top Norfolk Terrier in agility and, to date, the only Norfolk Terrier Agility Grand Champion. She is a Master Earthdog, as well as actually hunting on a regular basis on the farm where she lives. This is only one example among my many terrier students. Dogs are like people: let them do what they love, and they will appreciate you for it.

FRANKIE JOIRIS

The Benefits of Proper Training

Welsh Terriers of all ages can benefit from training. It helps your dog understand what you want and how to behave. The process can also teach you to read your Welshie's body language and better understand what motivates it.

Once you teach your dog what you want and encourage these behaviors, you won't have to say "no" very often. The improved communication between you and your pet builds trust and deepens the canine-human bond.

Training should give your terrier more confidence as well. Faced with an unfamiliar experience, a trained dog will trust your ability to lead the way. Should a situation turn dangerous, a Welshie's training may even

Photo Courtesy of Karen Yeomans

help keep it safe. For instance, if your dog gets loose, it's much more likely to come to you when called if trained to do so.

Training is also mentally stimulating for a Welsh Terrier. It can prevent boredom and help keep your dog happy. Practicing cognitive exercises indoors is a great outlet for a terrier's energy during inclement weather.

Taking Classes/Lessons vs. Sending Your Welshie to a Trainer

When you take private lessons or attend a group class with your Welsh Terrier, the trainer teaches you how to train the dog yourself. A good instructor guides you through the steps that help a Welshie understand what you want. The instructor explains what your dog is communicating through its body language. As you learn to teach specific exercises by breaking them down into small steps that build to a desired behavior, you gain an understanding of how to explain things to your dog. Under the watchful eye of an experienced trainer, you learn when and how to reward your Welshie's behavior and when to ignore it.

If you send your Welsh Terrier away to be trained by an experienced dog trainer, it will learn to obey that trainer, but you will miss out on bonding more closely with it through the training experience. You also won't learn how to explain things to your terrier or how to read its body language. A synopsis from the trainer of what your dog has learned does not prepare you to deal with lapses in training or other issues that may arise.

DID YOU KNOW?
Welsh Terrier Fire

Welsh Terriers exhibit a set of personality traits colloquially called "terrier fire." These feisty dogs are independent, intelligent, and brave. According to the AKC Welsh Terrier breed standard, these dogs should be "... alert, aware, spirited but at the same time, friendly and show self-control." This unique terrier fire is an asset, but can also translate to stubbornness. As a result, patience and consistency are crucial when training a Welsh Terrier.

Some behavioral problems arise because of issues specific to a dog's home environment. Sending a canine away to be trained will not fix these problems if the home environment does not improve and people in the home don't learn how to handle the dog.

You train your Welshie every day whether you intend to or not. For example, if your dog ignores you when you call it and you repeat the command instead of going to get the dog, you are teaching it that it's okay to ignore your command. A basic understanding of how your terrier learns will help you recognize and avoid some instances of unintentional training.

To live harmoniously with a Welshie, you should know how to explain things to it and understand what it is telling you. If you don't have these skills, find a talented trainer to teach you.

Choosing a Trainer

Dog training is an unregulated industry, which means there are no licensing or educational requirements for anyone calling themselves a professional dog trainer. Unfortunately, this allows unqualified people to advertise and provide their services to clients who don't know any better.

There are programs that provide training certification based mainly on online or written test results. While it is great to understand the theories of dog training, nothing can replace the hands-on experience of training multiple dogs. In my opinion, the experience of training many dogs of various breeds is what produces a good trainer.

When looking for a trainer, get referrals from knowledgeable dog people. Ask your breeder or rescue group for suggestions. Your veterinarian, local terrier breeders and owners, and area AKC clubs may also recommend good local trainers.

If someone has successfully trained a wide variety of dog breeds, their training methods probably work well with most dogs. I would look for someone with terrier experience or who has at least successfully taught owners of terriers. The titles earned by the trainer's dogs (and students' dogs) in competition are proof of the success of a training program. A title shows that multiple knowledgeable judges certified a dog's performance.

Look for a reward-based training program, and try to observe a class to see if the methods employed and the teacher's overall manner are right for you and your Welshie. Obviously, a trainer must know how to train a dog, but he/she must also communicate instructions to you in a way you understand and can explain to your terrier. I would never take lessons from a trainer who yells at students or dogs or hits dogs. You want to see owners and dogs working happily in class.

Questions to ask a trainer:

- How long have you been training?
- How did you learn to train dogs and their owners?
- Do you have experience with terriers?
- What have you accomplished as a trainer?

Age is another consideration when choosing a class. Look for a puppy class if your Welsh Terrier is less than five months old. For a dog that is five months or older, look for a regular obedience class. If your new terrier is a fully trained adult, consider yourself fortunate. An obedience class, trick class, or beginning agility class could still help strengthen the bond and communication between you and a trained Welshie, especially if you've never owned a terrier before.

Practice Matters

Photo Courtesy of Alyssa Teixeira

Attending a class once a week with your dog isn't likely to result in a well-trained dog. You need to help your Welsh Terrier with its homework to achieve success.

Things to consider for practice:

1. Keep practice sessions short. I have found training a Welshie for short periods several times a day works better than one long session.
2. Where you train matters. When first learning an exercise, it is easier for a terrier to focus with no distractions. After a dog learns to perform a task without distractions, gradually add more distractions one at a time. Begin with mild distractions and make them more exciting as your Welshie learns to ignore them. For example, the first distraction might be a stationary toy on the ground, and gradually, you can work up to a person running with a squeaky toy or several robotic stuffed toys barking and hopping nearby.
3. Timing is important. I don't train immediately after my dogs have eaten. Practicing before dinnertime when your terrier's stomach is empty can make your pet more eager to earn a reward. Also, feeding time is great for practicing "sit" and "wait/stay," as you can have your dog sit and wait before getting its food.

Behave Yourself

Be a calm and encouraging leader for your Welsh Terrier. Sometimes you may need to repeat an exercise many times before your dog figures out what you want. In these instances, remain calm and ignore the wrong choices your Welshie makes. Do not fuss, yell, or hit your terrier

Photo Courtesy of Marc Scholtyssek

for making a mistake in training. When your dog takes the desired action, reward it profusely. This is how your pet learns what you want and what doesn't earn a reward.

Stay the course with your Welsh Terrier's training and behavioral regimen. Don't let minor setbacks or inconveniences discourage your efforts. You must be more determined than your Welshie.

Be consistent. Otherwise, your terrier will be confused. All day, every day, reward good behavior, and try not to reward undesirable behaviors. Make sure everyone uses the same commands for your dog's behaviors.

Be patient. Dogs learn at different rates.

Be fair, and don't expect your Welshie to know something you haven't yet trained it to do.

Be flexible. When you or your Welshie have a bad day, it's okay to skip a practice session and enjoy some playtime or cuddle time instead.

Chapter 10: Training

Be proactive. Think about how you want your Welsh Terrier to behave and then help it achieve that goal. Don't wait until your pet develops some undesirable behaviors to start training it.

Don't give treats for free. Your dog should work for its treats so it understands that obedience pays.

Don't expect your Welsh Terrier to pay attention to you unless you pay attention to it. This breed craves attention from its owners.

Training Tips

Welsh Terriers are very smart and stubborn. They learn quickly, but don't enjoy obeying the same commands over and over unless they see something in it for them. Most love food rewards, while some respond better to toys. Praise and pets are always appreciated. Welsh Terriers can be very headstrong, so you need to teach them that you are the top dog, and discourage any excessive guarding of food, toys, or people.

EREIGN SEACORD
Esty Glen Welsh Terriers

1. Mistakes help your dog learn. Don't get upset or try to prevent your dog from making mistakes during training sessions. Your terrier needs to learn what behavior gets rewarded and what doesn't.
2. Make training fun for your dog. Use plenty of praise, treats, and toys to reward your Welshie's hard work.
3. Choose rewards your dog desires. Some dogs would rather work for toys than food, and others are the opposite. My dog Bear would practically turn inside out for bits of baby carrots, but I had another Welshie who initially preferred toys over treats.

Photo Courtesy of Michelle Apple

4. If you have an adult or teenaged terrier that is not well socialized, it may be best to start with a few private lessons before transitioning to a group class.
5. Make sure your dog gets enough exercise. It's hard for a terrier that is bursting with excess energy to focus on training.

CHAPTER 11

Basic Lessons

Successful dog training is a two-way conversation between human and dog. You explain to your Welsh Terrier what you want, your dog responds to you, and then you respond accordingly.

Sometimes you find a dog seems to have forgotten what you spent the past weeks training to perfection. There are different theories for why this happens. One theory holds that when this happens, a canine's brain is transferring what it learned from short-term memory to long-term memory. So don't despair; just back up a few training steps to the point your dog understands the lesson and continue working from there. This "forgotten" phase doesn't last long.

There are various positive methods of dog training that work well with Welsh Terriers. I'll share what has worked for me.

A few things I recommend when training:

1. Keep training sessions short (especially with young puppies) and quit before your Welshie loses interest. It is better to train a few minutes multiple times a day than to work your terrier for a long period. You can gradually increase training time as your dog learns to focus for longer periods.
2. Start teaching something new to your Welsh Terrier in a distraction-free environment in your home. As the dog learns, you can gradually add in distractions and train outside.
3. Canines can have difficulty understanding positions associated with commands. For instance, say you have taught your dog to reliably sit in front of you, but when you ask that dog to sit on your right or left side, it doesn't understand the sit command because the position has changed. It may think "sit" is something that it does in front of you. In this case, you must train your terrier (starting with a lure) to

sit in this new position. It goes much quicker in each subsequent position.
4. If you are training with treats, gradually lessen the number of times your Welshie gets a treat reward once it thoroughly understands an exercise. (You should still praise the dog every time.) To do this, give a treat every other time your terrier performs the command. Eventually, give your terrier a treat every third time it is correct. The goal is to reward your Welshie with a treat intermittently. This results in a dog conditioned to obey you happily for praise and with only intermittent treat rewards.

May I Have Your Attention, Please?

Before you can train a Welsh Terrier, you must have its attention. All Earthdog breeds can focus intensely. That trait was once necessary for doing battle with dangerous quarry underground in tight quarters in the dark. The trick is getting your dog to focus on you.

While some Welshies are naturally more attentive than others, all can learn to pay attention to their human. There is nothing magical about your terrier focusing on you. It results from a strong bond nurtured with treats, toys, fun training, gentle massages, enjoyable activities, and outings. There are ways to encourage your dog to pay attention to you, and you can even teach your dog to pay attention on cue.

One way to increase the attention your Welshie gives you is to praise and treat it for voluntarily focusing on you without stimulus. Keep an eye out for those times when you catch the dog randomly looking at you so you can reward the behavior.

You can also practice attention by saying your Welsh Terrier's name. When it responds by looking at you, make eye contact and lavishly reward your pet. Do this with a happy, smiling face because glaring unpleasantly into a dog's eyes may be interpreted as a challenge in dog language. (Avoid using your Welshie's name negatively, such as scolding. You want the terrier to associate positive experiences with its name.)

If your dog doesn't look at you when you say its name, don't repeat the name. Instead, make a weird sound that will get its attention and praise and treat when it looks at you. Eventually, your Welshie will look when you say its name without you having to make a weird noise.

If you want to delve further into attention work with your Welsh Terrier, there are many successful trainers in the United States teaching focused attention. I was fortunate to work with Diane Bauman, a well-known trainer, when I pursued more advanced obedience with my dog Bear.

The first thing I learned was how to teach Bear a release or "at ease" command from a commanded sit. Then Bauman had me stand still with Bear sitting beside me and begin teaching my sitting dog to watch me on command. After perfecting stationary attention on cue with no distractions, we added distractions. Finally, after practicing at home, Bear and I were ready to learn to heel with focused attention. We started with just a few steps at a time.

Eventually, I competed in the obedience ring with my Welshie and earned near-perfect scores. Best of all, this attention work made my bond with Bear even stronger. (A little caveat about attention on cue: You need to teach your terrier a release or "at ease" command to go with the attention command. Focused attention is very tiring and should only be asked of a dog for short periods of time.)

Coming When Called

One of the first things you should work on with any new dog is coming when called. This command could be a lifesaver someday, so practice it throughout a terrier's life. Don't use an extremely narrow collar to train/practice recalls, as it could place stress on your terrier's neck if you need to give a gentle tug. I like to use a wide martingale collar for this.

First, choose one command for the recall that everyone in the household will use. It could be "come" or "here" or another word that is short and simple. Whatever word you choose, only use it for positive experiences. If your dog learned to ignore the command "come" prior to joining your family, use a different word for the command.

Never call your Welshie to you in an angry voice or for punishment. That will eventually teach it not to come when called.

I like to start indoors in a distraction-free room with a game using high-value rewards (either food or favorite toys). You can find various recall training games online. The one I like the best with a new Welsh Terrier requires two people. Both people sit on the floor facing each other about eight to ten feet apart. One person holds the dog while the other person talks excitedly to it without using its name or the command to come. They can make funny noises, clap, or wave a toy to make the terrier

> **DID YOU KNOW?**
> **Dog Sports for Welsh Terriers**
>
> Welsh Terriers were initially bred to hunt and kill small animals, such as foxes, badgers, and rodents. The echoes of this heritage can be seen in this breed today in the form of a strong prey drive and high energy levels. As a result of these traits, Welsh Terriers often excel at dog sports that utilize their instincts for hunting. Therefore, the AKC suggests Barn Hunt, Earthdog, and Coursing Ability Tests as particularly suitable for Welsh Terriers. For more information about these dog sports, visit www.akc.org/sports.

want to come to them. Once the Welshie is focused on and excited about going to that person, he/she should say the dog's name and give the recall command. As soon as the recall command is given, the individual holding the dog should let it loose to run to the other person.

When the Welsh Terrier reaches the person who called the dog, he/she should praise the dog while holding the reward (treat or toy) in front of its nose and taking hold of the collar gently. Once the collar is held, the Welshie gets the reward. Make a big fuss over the dog to reinforce that coming when called is one of the most pleasurable things it can do.

Now you can reverse the game and have the other person call the dog. Play the game for a few rounds, but stop before your terrier gets bored. After the dog has learned to play the game indoors, you can take it outside. You can also increase the distance and stand up. To increase the speed of your Welshie's recall, you can call your dog to come and then run away or quickly back away from it. Having the terrier chase you makes the recall a little more exciting. It's also a good way to catch a loose dog.

Teach your dog to come close to you, whether in front of you or beside you, and always insist that you have your hand on the collar

Photo Courtesy of Karen Yeomans

before it receives the reward. If you don't have a fenced-in yard, you can train the recall on a long line (at least 15 feet).

Never reward a Welsh Terrier for not coming when called. You want to show your pet that it doesn't have any option except to come. You also don't want to run toward a Welshie you are trying to catch. Running toward a dog will most likely cause it to run away from you.

Without a helper, you can put your terrier on a leash inside the house (without distractions). Call your dog from short distances. Again, when the Welsh Terrier comes, you will hold a treat or toy in front of its nose with one hand while your other hand gently takes its collar. Once the collar is grasped, your terrier gets its reward. Gradually increase the distance of the recall and, as your Welshie progresses, add in some distractions. If the dog ignores your command, you can give a gentle tug on the leash to encourage it to come. (This is not a punishment. It is a gentle reminder to listen to you.) Do not repeat your command.

When your dog understands the recall indoors, move the lesson outside with your dog on a ten-foot leash, starting with short distances. If you have a fenced-in yard, you can drop the leash and pick it up if you need to give a gentle tug if your dog ignores your recall command. If you don't have a fenced-in yard, don't drop the leash. As always, start with few to no distractions and gradually add them in as your dog progresses. With a 20-foot-long line on your dog, you can start practicing recalls from a greater distance.

You should always praise and pet your dog effusively for coming when called, but you can gradually work toward rewarding only intermittently with a toy or treat. Eventually, you will always praise and pet for a recall, but only occasionally give a treat or toy.

Whenever your dog is off-leash in the house or in the yard and ignores your recall command, don't repeat the command. (If you repeat a command that was not obeyed, you are teaching your dog to ignore you.) Go get your terrier instead of repeating the command. Maintain a calm demeanor, and don't be rough. Walk slowly and silently to catch your Welshie, take its collar, and then slowly and silently walk it back to the spot you called from. When you reach that spot, cheerfully say, "Good dog," but don't give a treat or toy before releasing it. This is not punishment. You are helping the dog to understand that coming when called is not optional.

Sit and Release

In the beginning, I teach a sit with the dog standing in front of me. Holding a cookie in both hands, place your left hand just in front of the Welsh Terrier's nose so it can smell the treat. Next, slowly raise the cookie in an arc up and over the dog's head. Be careful not to hold the treat too high because that will encourage your terrier to jump up instead of sitting. The dog's nose will naturally follow the cookie upward, and when its nose goes up, its bottom should go down. Now you have a sitting Welsh Terrier. Say "good" and reward the dog with the cookie in your right hand, but don't give the cookie in your left hand. You are luring your pet into position with a cookie. Don't give a command yet. Practice until the dog is reliably following the lure into a sit position.

If your Welsh Terrier doesn't go into the sit for the food lure, you can put the leash on and help guide it into position. Hold the leash in your right hand, and as you lure the dog with your left hand, gently pull up and back (diagonally) on the leash to encourage it to move its front end up and back so that its hind end sits on the floor.

Gradually increase the time that you expect your Welshie to sit before it gets its cookie. In the beginning, give the treat immediately. Next, give it after a momentary pause. Then, count to three in your head and give the cookie. Eventually, you can count to ten before giving your Welshie the cookie. If the dog's butt comes off the floor before you reward it, shorten the time between the treat and the sit and then gradually try to stretch out the time again. I occasionally give a second cookie a few seconds later, so long as the Welshie's butt stays on the floor.

When your terrier is used to following your left hand and being rewarded with your right hand, stop holding food in your left hand but continue to use it as a lure. (Eventually, the hand signal for a sit can be raising your left hand with the palm up in front of you with the elbow at your side, but for now, that hand is still a lure.)

Once the dog has mastered the previous step, add in your verbal command. I say "sit" before I raise my left hand to lure the sit. Continue luring with the left hand and rewarding with your right hand. At some point, your Welshie will start sitting when you say "sit" before you even raise your hand. Soon you will be able to ask your terrier to "sit" without the lure.

At the same time you begin using the verbal "sit" command, start giving your dog a release command such as "free" to signal when it is released from the sit. Say "free" in a cheerful, excited voice while standing up straight. You can even raise your hands and give a little clap to encourage your Welsh Terrier to move out of the sit.

If the dog pops up before you release it, use the leash to guide it back into the sit by gently pulling diagonally (up and back). This should guide the Welshie back into a sit without repeating the command. Now you can say "good" and then release the terrier from the sit.

Chapter 11: Basic Lessons

Keep the sits very short for all ages of dogs initially. With puppies and high-energy teenagers, be very gradual when increasing the time you expect a dog to sit. (I use a stay command when I want a terrier to hold a position for more than a couple of minutes.) You can play with your dog for a few moments after you give the release command.

Photo Courtesy of Lisa Tucker

Once the Welshie has mastered sitting with a verbal command, you can start practicing with distractions. Whenever your dog ignores the "sit" command, use the same very gentle upward tug of the leash to remind it to obey. As soon as the dog is sitting, say, "Good."

You can also start asking for sits beside you rather than in front of you. If your dog doesn't understand that "sit" means it should sit beside you the same as it did in front of you, take a step back in the training and lure it into a sit beside you.

As the dog becomes more proficient, add in distractions and start practicing outdoors. The goal is a dog that will reliably sit on command in any situation.

If you want to teach a hand signal for the sit, you can gradually transition from luring with the left hand to simply raising the hand with the palm up. After the Welshie has learned both verbal and hand signals, you can alternate their use in practice to ensure the dog will respond to one without the other. Hand signals can come in very handy if a dog goes deaf in its old age. I have a friend whose 17-year-old Welshie has lost its hearing in old age and works entirely with hand signals.

Walking On-leash

There are two important things you need to teach your Welsh Terrier about walking on-leash:

1. Walking beside you is a very pleasant and rewarding experience.
2. The reward zone when walking on lead is always near you and very slightly in front of your leg on the side the terrier is walking as it faces the same direction as you. The reward zone for close leash-walking is NOT several steps in front of you, behind you, or way out to the side.

With a puppy that is not used to a collar, harness, or leash, start by placing the collar or harness on the youngster indoors and letting it walk around for a short, supervised period of time to get used to it. (I recommend using a martingale collar to leash train a young puppy. It's much less likely to slip off over a small puppy head than a regular flat collar and is less of a distraction than a harness with many parts.) Once a pup is used to its collar or harness, attach a leash and let it drag the leash around inside for a brief time under your supervision.

Photo Courtesy of Hayley Rampton

Chapter 11: Basic Lessons

When your puppy is comfortable wearing a leash and collar, you can pick up the leash and follow your puppy. Yes, that's right. Let your Welshie lead you both indoors and outdoors. You will, of course, be armed with treats and toys so you can lure the youngster away from somewhere it shouldn't go. Trail your puppy closely as it sniffs and explores the world. Anytime your terrier looks at you or allows you to lure it in a different direction, praise and reward it.

I like to teach a young puppy to walk beside me, off-leash, before doing it on-leash. You can start in an enclosed area with all toys and distractions removed. (For very distractible Welshies, starting indoors is easiest.) You will need a pocketful of high-value, pea-sized treats. (If your dog isn't interested in food, you can do this with its favorite small toys, but food treats are preferable for this work.) My method can also be helpful in retraining an adult that doesn't have a clue how to behave on lead.

To begin, call your Welsh Terrier to your preferred side. Always start by teaching your dog to walk on a particular side. Once it has figured out how to walk on your preferred side, you can teach it to walk on the opposite side, following the same steps but using a different command. It can be useful to have a terrier that will walk comfortably on either side. There may be times when it is preferable to have your Welshie change sides on a walk.

When the dog is beside you, facing the same direction as you, say "good" and give a treat from your hand with your palm toward the terrier. Then hold another treat just slightly above and in front of your Welshie's nose, give the walk command, such as "let's go," and take one step. (Don't hold the treat too high or too far ahead.) As soon as your puppy has walked with you for one step, say "good" and reward, then give the release command. Wait a few minutes and then repeat. Once your terrier has mastered walking one step beside you, add another step before you praise, reward, and then release. You can gradually increase the steps until your pup reliably follows the food for ten steps. At this point, your Welshie is ready to follow the treat beside you as you turn right or left.

Next, you can add the leash. Hold the leash in the hand opposite the side the dog is walking on. Hold the cookie in the hand nearest the dog. Start with one step and gradually add more steps before the reward, followed by a release. Early on, if I am working in an enclosed area, I drop the

Photo Courtesy of Linda Brisbin

leash after the release command. This prevents the terrier from pulling on the leash when you are not working on walking close to you.

When your Welshie has mastered walking beside you indoors, you can move outside somewhere with few or no distractions and repeat the lessons. (Make sure your dog goes potty before you start.) As your puppy becomes skilled at walking beside you, add in a few distractions; just make sure you have very high-value treats that will hold its attention. Start with a few steps, and add more as your Welshie becomes more proficient. If your terrier looks away at a distraction, you can tap him gently on the nose with the cookie or make a weird sound as you waggle the cookie to remind him that you have something more interesting.

Having your Welshie walk close beside you is not something you should require for long periods of time. It will be much more pleasant for your terrier if you allow it to walk on a somewhat longer leash and don't always require it to be next to you. When walking on a longer leash, allow your dog to sniff, roll in the grass, etc., so long as it doesn't pull on the leash and keeps up with you.

If your Welshie pulls on the leash, turn in the opposite direction, give the command for walking close to you, and start walking. Wait until the dog has taken a few steps beside you before rewarding it. Repeat this anytime your terrier pulls, and it will eventually figure out that pulling doesn't get it where it wants to go.

Another way to deal with a dog pulling is simply to stand still until it stops pulling. In my experience, Welshies learn not to pull quicker with the turning and walking in the opposite direction method.

I keep sessions short when working on something new, especially with puppies. Young terriers have a limited ability to focus and self-control. Stop training before they lose interest.

It is also a good idea to make sure a puppy or high-energy adult has had some exercise and gone potty before a leash-training session. It's easier for them to focus with a little less pent-up energy and an empty bladder.

Stand

It is easy to teach a dog to stand from a sit or down position. You just hold food in front of its nose and lure it forward into the standing position with the food. Once your Welshie stands, say "good" and reward and then release. After the dog is reliably following the lure, start using a verbal command just before luring it forward.

Down

I teach my Welsh Terriers to lie down from a standing position. You can teach this from a sit, but it seems to confuse canines. Have you ever seen a dog that was commanded "down" and sat instead? Sometimes a dog will sit for a few moments and then lie down. I prefer to skip all that confusion and go straight to the "down" position from standing when training.

With the terrier standing either beside you or in front of you, hold a cookie in your right hand up to the dog's nose. Then slowly take your hand down to the floor, going slightly toward your Welshie's front legs. As your terrier follows the treat in your hand, it will probably lie down. As soon as it does, say "good" and give a reward.

For a Welsh Terrier that refuses to lie down for a lure, you can use the capture method to teach "down." (The "down" position is very submissive for dogs, and some may be wary of being asked to perform this position.) Anytime you see your dog lie down on its own, say "good" and give a treat as soon as the Welshie is completely in the down position.

Eventually, your dog will figure out that lying down gets rewarded, and it will start offering the behavior to get a treat. Now, put the Welshie on a six-foot leash, show it you have a cookie, and wait. It should start to offer different behaviors to get the treat. When it lies down, give it the treat. Once the dog offers the "down" on-leash regularly, add in the verbal command "down."

When you start giving the verbal command, it's also time to start using the release command at the end of the exercise. If you have trouble getting your pet to stay down for more than half a second, try giving it more than one treat as it remains in the down position.

For a Welshie that is very insistent on popping up almost as soon as its elbows hit the floor, you can gently press down on the shoulders (across the withers) to guide the dog back into the down position when you see its elbows starting to come off the floor. Don't repeat the "down" command. You're temporarily holding your terrier in position. This is not a punishment, so don't be rough. The dog may resist, but as soon as it relaxes in the down position, say, "Good." Wait a second, and then give the release command.

Stay

Even though I expect my Welsh Terriers to hold a position until I give the release command, I teach "stay" for when I may be out of sight or want the dog to stay in position longer than a few minutes.

You can teach your Welsh Terrier to stay in a sit, stand, and down position. The dog needs to know the command for the position you intend to use and understand the release command before you train a stay.

Choose either the sit or down position (whichever seems the most comfortable for the Welshie) for the initial training. Your dog can start on a six-foot leash, and as the training progresses and you can move further away from your Welsh Terrier, switch to a longer line.

For the sit/stay, hold the leash in your right hand and ask the terrier to sit on your left side. Once it is sitting, hold your left hand open with a flat palm facing the dog in front of your dog's nose without touching it. Wait a second and then say, "Stay." Remove your hand signal. Then slowly take one step forward with your right foot. (In formal obedience training, stepping off with the foot beside your dog is a cue for the animal to move.

Stepping off with the foot away from the dog is a cue for it to stay.) Now, step back into your original position.

If your Welshie remains sitting for this exercise, say "good" and give a treat. (The terrier should remain sitting while being praised and rewarded. Don't be so effusive in your praise that your dog gets excited and jumps up.) Next, give your dog the release command.

If your terrier stands up or lies down before the release, move back to your original position and put your pet back into a sit using the leash. Don't scold your Welshie or push it into a sit with your hand. When it is sitting, say "good," but don't give a second command. A simple "good" tells your dog it is in the desired position. Again, step forward and then back. If the dog gets up again, repeat this process until it stays.

I used to have a terrible habit of trying to help my Welshie by softly scolding "ah, ah" if it looked like it was thinking about breaking a stay. This didn't help the dog learn the "stay" command. My trainer Diane Bauman taught me that a dog will have a clearer understanding if you allow it to make mistakes and then show it what you want. "Helping" my pet avoid making mistakes only made it harder for the dog to learn the exercise.

Eventually, you will walk all the way around your terrier and also increase the distance you walk away from it during a sit/stay. As your dog progresses, you can add in distractions and ask for a sit/stay from other positions, such as in front of you.

You can use the same method for teaching down/stay and stand/stay.

Leave It

Use the command "leave it" when you want your Welsh Terrier to leave something alone or ignore something very tempting. To teach this command, put the terrier on a leash and place something it will want a short distance away from it. Tell your dog to "leave it," and if it ignores the object, say "good" and give it a treat. If your dog tries to approach the object after your "leave it" command, pick up the object (without allowing your dog to take hold of it) and ignore your dog. Practice this with different tempting objects, and eventually, your Welsh Terrier will learn to "leave it." If necessary, you can give a gentle tug on the leash after telling

Photo Courtesy of Jane Latheron

your dog to "leave it." There is no need to yell if it makes the wrong choice during training. Ignoring your terrier's wrong choices and rewarding the correct choices should be enough (along with an occasional leash tug) to teach this command.

Drop It

Train your dog to drop what it has in its mouth using the "drop it" command. Use a toy your Welshie likes and willingly carries in its mouth to teach "drop it," but not its favorite toy. Encourage it to grab the toy. When the terrier has the toy in its mouth, say "drop it" and hold a very high-value treat under the dog's nose. As soon as it drops the toy, say "good" and give it the cookie. While the terrier gulps down the cookie, pick up the toy and hold it behind your back. Repeat this process three or four times several times a day. As your dog learns to "drop it," slowly increase the value of the toy you are asking it to drop. When your Welshie is proficiently performing this command, you can gradually wean it to intermittent treat rewards.

Tricks

I think tricks should be part of basic training for terriers. Tricks are fun and can help your Welshie focus on you in stressful situations. I ask a Welsh Terrier to "wave" and "beg" in veterinary office waiting rooms if someone else's pet is being very disruptive. I explain in Chapter 9 how I use a particular trick to keep a dog focused on me when walking by a major distraction. There are many good online articles and YouTube videos that teach how to train your dog tricks. Frankie Joiris, a professional animal trainer I have worked with, offers a Trick Dog online class and a Star Dog online class (for training like a movie star dog) at her website https://dogpotentialunleashed.com/. She taught me how to teach my dogs tricks I never dreamed of.

CHAPTER 12

Behavioral Issues

Welsh Terriers are highly prey-driven. If it's moving, it's got their attention. This could be your cat, the neighbor's small dog, a piece of paper blowing across the ground, or even a small child. Potential Welsh Terrier owners need to understand that these dogs were bred for a purpose: to be tasked with going down dark holes after unknown prey.

EMILY CARROLL
Bayleigh Carroway Welsh Terriers

Everyone wants a well-behaved dog, but at some point in every dog's life, it will behave in an undesirable way. When this happens, stay calm and try to figure out what is causing the inappropriate behavior. In my experience, there are a variety of reasons that Welshies misbehave, including:

- Health issues
- Changes in routine
- Not enough exercise
- Boredom
- Lack of training/poor socialization
- Instinct
- Natural stages of a dog's life (such as fear periods)
- Reinforced misbehavior

Chapter 12 : Behavioral Issues

If your Welsh Terrier's behavior changes suddenly, take it to your vet to make sure there is no underlying health issue. Medical problems can cause things like using the bathroom in the house, anxiety, fear, and aggression. Pain can cause a dog to become irritable and even aggressive.

Figuring out the root cause of your Welshie's inappropriate behavior helps you change it. For instance, a very young or old terrier may not be capable of waiting long periods of time between bathroom breaks. So, you may need to schedule more trips outside. (With a young puppy, physical maturity and proper training will eventually allow it to wait longer to go potty.)

HELPFUL TIP

A Dirty Habit – Digging

Welsh Terriers are no more likely to dig than any other breed. The following are a few tips for diminishing a digging habit and preventing damage to your yard:
- Tire your Welshie out with plenty of **exercise**
- Provide plenty of toys for mental stimulation
- Bury chicken wire or other **dig deterrents** in popular digging spots and beneath fences
- Some dogs dig to find a cool place to sleep, so provide **plenty of shade and water** in the warm months

Another example is when your terrier pesters you for food while you eat. If you ignore these annoying entreaties, a Welshie learns quickly this harassment doesn't work. However, if you give in just once, you are teaching your dog this behavior gets rewarded. Once learned, you can untrain the irritating habit by ignoring your dog when it pesters you. Unfortunately, it takes much longer for a terrier to unlearn the habit after it's been rewarded than discouraging it in the first place.

Living with a Teenage Welsh Terrier

A teenage Welsh Terrier will typically become more independent, test boundaries to figure out what it can get away with, and need plenty of exercise. You must be patient, use common sense, and carry on with training and reinforcing desired behaviors. Sometimes, a teenage terrier may seem to forget previous lessons. Just take your training a few steps back and reteach any forgotten lessons. Remember, this stage will pass. (See Chapter 2 for more information on the adolescent period.)

Chewing

It's natural for dogs to chew, so you don't want to stop your Welsh Terrier from chewing. Instead, redirect it to chew on appropriate items. Try to have many chew types of toys at home so you can provide your Welshie with a variety. I make sure a dog always has at least two different chew toys available in case it gets bored with one of them.

Puppies are indiscriminate chewers as they explore the world with their teeth. At around three months old, a Welsh Terrier will start to lose its baby teeth as its adult teeth grow in. During teething, a youngster will chew on things to make its gums feel better. You must puppy-proof your home to make sure a young Welsh Terrier doesn't have access to things you don't want it to chew, especially when you are not supervising. Make sure a puppy always has several approved items to chew.

Photo Courtesy of Alyssa Teixeira

When you see your terrier chew on something inappropriate, say "leave it" (if the item is not carried in its mouth) or "drop it" (if the item is carried in its mouth), and then offer your dog a more attractive chew toy to chomp on. Praise your pet when it chews on the offered chew toy.

Sometimes a dog chews because of separation anxiety. In that situation, you need to keep a terrier enclosed in a puppy-proof environment with plenty of chew toys when you are not home. That may mean crating your pet. You also must help your dog get over its separation anxiety.

Biting

All dogs bite. They bite their food when they eat. They may bite prey when they hunt. They bite other dogs (lightly) and their toys when they play. A canine may also bite out of fear, aggression, or pain.

A puppy explores the world with its teeth, and that includes nipping the hands and feet of people until it learns better. Puppies get their first lessons in bite inhibition from their mother and littermates. In these early lessons, a puppy learns not to bite too hard. For instance, when a young Welsh Terrier bites too hard, its littermate yelps in pain and briefly stops playing. Over time, the puppy learns to bite its littermates more softly. If the youngster bites its mom too hard, the discipline will be swift and possibly a little tougher than what its littermates dish out.

This training must continue with the breeder and owners of a young Welsh Terrier. When a puppy bites, it's best to react like a littermate and give a loud, sharp yelp or "ouch" and then ignore the puppy for 30 seconds. After, you can offer your terrier a toy and continue to play with it. The toy should be large enough that you and the youngster can hold it at the same time without your hand being near the puppy's mouth.

If a puppy is hyper-aroused or overtired, the yelp method alone won't work. You may need to walk out of the room to give an overexcited youngster the opportunity to calm down for a few minutes. It will eventually learn that nipping when overexcited ends play. An exhausted pup may need to be crated or left alone in an enclosed area to rest.

The goal is to train your young Welshie in a way it can understand not to bite humans and teach it what it's allowed to bite. This doesn't happen overnight, and it requires that everyone playing with the puppy adhere to the program. This method does not involve verbal or physical punishment.

You will also need to make sure your puppy always has puppy chews and toys that it can safely sink its teeth into. A young Welshie should also have a chew toy in its crate.

One of the best ways to prevent a puppy from growing up to be a fear biter is to socialize it. (See Chapter 9 for information on socialization.) Even if you have a full-grown Welsh Terrier that was never socialized, you can still work on adult socialization to help desensitize it to some things.

Photo Courtesy of Hayley Rampton

Training your Welsh Terrier decreases the chances that it will grow up to be a biter. When you teach your pet how to behave and condition it to want to behave, life is so much easier for both of you.

If you have a Welshie that threatens to bite when you attempt to take something away from it, work on the "drop it" and "leave it" commands discussed in Chapter 11. Remember, you must teach your terrier how you want it to behave because it is not born knowing how to be the perfect pet.

If you have an adult Welsh Terrier that bites people, reach out to experts for help. Talk to your veterinarian to rule out physical problems. Contact your breeder and/or WTCARES at https://welshterrierrescue.com/ for advice and suggestions on trainers/behaviorists. (WTCARES is a great resource when dealing with behavioral problems in Welsh Terriers.)

Biting is not a breed-specific problem but a problem that occurs in individual dogs of all types for various reasons. It can be a serious situation that requires expert attention, preferably from someone who has experience with terriers. (Avoid anyone who wants you to dominate your pet with force. This method can create fear and amplify aggression in a dog.) Don't be ashamed to ask for help.

There are rare instances when an adult Welsh Terrier bites people and the safest option is to euthanize the dog. This is a decision that should be made in consultation with experts. You will have to decide if this is a situation where euthanasia is the only suitable solution. Some biting problems with adult dogs may have other solutions. One such situation is when a Welshie is so fearful of nail trimming that it growls and nips, but only during nail clipping. This pet doesn't pose a threat outside of nail trimming. It may be taught to be less stressed about nail trimming or can be muzzled for the procedure.

Chapter 12 : Behavioral Issues

Growling: Listen, Don't Scold

Photo Courtesy of Patricia Mast

Growling is one way a Welsh Terrier communicates, and it has a variety of growls that express different things. The play growl tells you that a Welshie is having fun. The talkative, happy growl (such as during a tummy rub) expresses pleasure like a cat purr.

There is also a frustration growl that is like a person grumbling about something annoying, such as a fence or leash preventing your dog from greeting a favorite person or a dog walking past. If you hear the frustration growl during training, you need to find a way to end the session on a positive note with an exercise that is easy for your dog. Afterward, consider whether the training drill that frustrated your dog needs to be broken into easier, simpler steps for future success.

Then there are warning growls. These growls are your Welsh Terrier's early warning system, alerting you that the dog is feeling afraid, stressed, possessive, aggressive, or in pain. To prevent the situation from escalating, you need to listen to your pet and figure out why it's warning you. Knowing the root cause of your terrier's warning growls can provide a blueprint for training or treatment to help your pet avoid this feeling in the future.

You should never reprimand a dog for growling. Instead, listen, respond, and be glad that your Welsh Terrier communicates with you.

Resource Guarding

Resource guarding occurs when a dog is overly protective of something highly valued, such as food, a spot on the couch, a toy, or even a person. A Welsh Terrier will give aggressive warnings if you approach it while it is guarding a valued possession. This behavior can occur in any type of dog.

Do not use force to deal with this issue. That could lead to an escalation. The best way to prevent this problem from developing is to teach a puppy to "leave it" and "drop it" and practice these commands throughout your pet's life. (See Chapter 11 for information on training "leave it" and "drop it.") Good socialization and basic training can prevent your pet from becoming possessive of the humans in its life. If you allow your terrier on the furniture, teach it a command that invites it onto your furniture, and teach an off command to prevent it from guarding a favorite spot.

I always drop high-value treats in my puppies' dishes when they eat. This teaches a youngster that it's okay for someone to mess with its dish even as it eats. Never chase a dog that has something you want. That will only escalate its guarding behavior.

When it is urgent to take something your Welshie is holding in its mouth and guarding, first try to distract it with a treat of very high value. Hopefully it will drop the object and take the treat. If that fails, pretend you are going for a walk and call your dog to the door with a leash and treats in hand. After attaching the leash, ask the terrier to "drop it" and then offer a cookie as a reward and retrieve the item. If your dog doesn't know "drop it," ask it to "sit" and offer a delicious reward when it does. Your dog should drop the item from its mouth to take the treat.

If your new Welsh Terrier is already exhibiting resource-guarding behavior, you can still teach "drop it" and "leave it." In addition, work with a good trainer or behaviorist to change this conduct. Behavior modification can be achieved in many dogs with this problem, but it often requires guidance from an expert experienced with positive training methods for this issue. It is important to address this problem before it gets worse.

Some dogs may have been so traumatized in the past that their resource-guarding behavior cannot be successfully modified. After consulting with experts in these instances, you may develop a workaround for the circumstances that cause your dog to resource guard. (I only suggest this for circumstances where the guarding behavior can be contained in a way that no people or pets can be threatened or harmed.)

My parents once took back an Irish Terrier they'd sold to someone who fed all his hounds and this lone terrier puppy out of one big trough.

Chapter 12 : Behavioral Issues

The hounds wouldn't let the puppy eat, so the starving puppy became aggressive with the hounds to get some food. The owner beat the puppy to teach it not to attack the hounds. Eventually, the dog was returned, but by then, it aggressively guarded its food dish. Behavior modification didn't work for this extremely traumatized dog, but my family could feed the dog in a room by itself, so that was never a problem. (The rest of its life was very pleasant.)

The Incorrigible People-Jumper

I described a method for teaching a Welsh Terrier to greet people in Chapter 9. If you've tried this and your adult dog is still an incorrigible people-jumper, there is another method that should work.

When I was a young child, my mother and I visited some people who owned an overly friendly adult dog that was an incorrigible

Photo Courtesy of Rhonda Metcalf

people-jumper. When this pet tried to put its front paws on my mother, she held them in her hands while she sweetly talked to the animal. She continued to hold its paws for several minutes, all the while speaking to it in a kind voice. The canine became uncomfortable, but my mother continued. Eventually, she let go of the dog's paws and petted it when its paws were on the ground. This dog never offered to jump on my mother again during the visit.

I was young and didn't understand what I witnessed my mother doing with this pet. Years later, I observed my trainer Diane Bauman doing the same thing with an adult dog, and she explained the technique to me. (There is also a detailed explanation on Bauman's website.)

This should only be done with a smart and people-friendly adult Welsh Terrier. The method will help a pet decide on its own that jumping on humans is not fun. When you employ this method, you must maintain a cheerful face and speak sweetly to the dog. Don't tell the terrier it's "good" because you don't want to praise the behavior, but don't yell at or scold the dog either. Just make very pleasant small talk with your prisoner.

A Welshie will struggle in this position and may even try to chew its way to freedom. If it chews, just hold the paws away from its mouth. After your terrier struggles for a few moments, release it, and as soon as all paws are on the floor, praise and pet.

For this method to succeed, the rest of the family and a few friends should do it as well. Don't try this with a dog that is young or not well-socialized. The paw-holding method is only for very people-friendly adult Welsh Terriers that don't mind being touched.

Barking

Barking is one way that dogs communicate, and they do it for many reasons, including excitement, attention-seeking, boredom, and fright. I have never found Welsh Terriers to be particularly yappy. However, for various reasons, any dog may become an excessive and/or nuisance barker, and there are things you can do to prevent it or solve the problem once started.

Chapter 12 : Behavioral Issues

Photo Courtesy of Veronika Holásková

1. Socialization. A well-socialized dog is less likely to bark from stress or excitement when it sees dogs or people.
2. Training. Train your Welshie how to behave, and ignore unwanted behavior. For instance, teach your dog to go to its bed or safe space when the doorbell rings. It can also be useful to teach a dog to speak on command and then teach it to be quiet on command.
3. Manage your Welsh Terrier. Make sure your dog gets enough exercise and is not left outside alone for too long. (Welshies crave companionship.)
4. Manage your terrier's spaces. Make sure all the areas your pet inhabits have a variety of toys to prevent boredom and keep the dog occupied. Close the curtains or place your pet in a room with limited window access when you are not at home so it won't be stimulated to bark by sights outside the house. For some Welshies, it may help to leave a radio or TV on to drown out noise coming from outside the home. A solid fence can limit a terrier's vision of people and animals outside your yard.
5. Desensitization to stimuli. You can practice various training exercises with your Welshie focused on you as people walk past

your yard. Your will learn to ignore these outside stimuli as it focuses on you.
6. Make sure you aren't unintentionally rewarding unwanted barking.
7. Consult an experienced trainer if you have trouble solving a barking problem.

Finally, some Welsh Terrier owners and fanciers seem to have the mistaken belief that allowing a Welshie to take part in Earthdog trials will teach it to bark or dig. That is ridiculous. Many of my Welsh Terriers have been involved in Earthdog trials, and every one of them knew how to bark before entering an Earthdog den. None of my Welshies ever barked more frequently or dug at home after participating in an Earthdog trial. These events give our terriers a unique outlet to enjoy their prey drive and don't encourage barking or digging in everyday life.

Digging

The Welsh Terriers I have known have not been prone to digging in the yard. I think there are three reasons a Welshie may dig.

1. Trying to reach something on the other side of the fence. I discuss a workable solution to this problem in Chapter 4.
2. Boredom. This shouldn't be a problem if you provide your dog with a wide variety of toys outdoors and don't leave it outside alone for hours at a time.
3. Vermin underground. If you have vermin tunneling underground, this issue might tempt any dog to dig. My mother had a German Shepherd that used to dig moles out of the ground.

Separation Anxiety

A Welsh Terrier that experiences extreme anxiety when left alone is suffering from separation anxiety. Manifestations of this problem can include extreme barking, destructive behavior, and going to the bathroom in the home.

Chapter 12 : Behavioral Issues

The best way to deal with this problem is to prevent your terrier from developing it. In Chapter 5, I suggested you acclimate your Welshie to being left alone, beginning on its very first day in your home. Leave your dog alone in its crate or safe space with chew toys (a Kong toy stuffed with an edible pet treat is a superb choice) while you go out of the house for just a few minutes.

Increase the time you are away gradually, and never make a big deal of saying goodbye when you leave or hello when you return. In a best-case scenario, your pet doesn't even notice when you go out the door and is happy when you return, but not overwhelmingly so.

Mental and physical exercise can also help relax a dog. So, make sure your Welshie is getting enough exercise.

What you don't want to do is spend every second with your pet and then one day suddenly disappear for hours. You need to prepare the dog for your absence.

If your Welsh Terrier is exhibiting mild signs of separation anxiety, you need to follow the same steps. Start by leaving the Welshie alone for just a few moments and then gradually increase the time. Let your dog tell you when to increase the alone time or if you need to back up temporarily to a shorter time.

For a terrier with a severe case of separation anxiety, speak to an expert, such as your breeder, veterinarian, or trainer/behaviorist, for guidance. Welsh Terriers are very social animals and should not be expected to spend most of their time alone. They need more than just a few minutes of your attention a day to thrive.

When You Need Help

If you can't solve your Welsh Terrier's behavioral problem on your own, get help from an expert. There is no shame in asking for help, and it's better to do it sooner than later. If you have an adult dog that bites, I strongly urge seeking expert help immediately.

Many dog trainers are skilled at dealing with behavioral issues, and Chapter 10 addresses how to choose a trainer. There are also applied animal behaviorists (who have advanced degrees in animal behavior from universities) and veterinary behaviorists (veterinarians with special training and certification in animal behavior who can prescribe medications for pets). Behaviorists are not trainers, but they help with behavior modification.

If You Don't Want or Can't Keep Your Welsh Terrier

Sometimes a Welsh Terrier ends up in a home where it's not a good fit. This happens. It doesn't mean the people are bad or the dog is bad. It just means they are not happy together. Maybe there isn't enough time for the dog, or behavioral issues are proving difficult to solve in the current situation. There are also occasions when a family can no longer keep their Welsh Terrier because of health or financial problems. The dog is loved, but circumstances require a new home for it. (I placed some of my dogs after a divorce, two strokes, and an autoimmune disease that compromised my health and my finances.)

If you don't want your Welsh Terrier or can no longer keep it, contact your breeder. Most responsible breeders will take a dog back at any point in its life. Your contract/agreement may also require that you return the dog if you can no longer keep it. (Some breeders will allow you to rehome a dog if they pre-approve the new home.)

A good breeder will not shame you for returning a dog. They will want to know the reason you don't want your Welshie. If your breeder thinks your situation isn't hopeless, they may offer advice for dealing with the terrier. Whether they help you solve an issue so you can keep your dog, help you rehome it, or take it back, a good breeder will treat you with courtesy. So don't be afraid to contact them.

Breeders love the terriers they breed and continue to care about them after they have gone to new homes. Don't blame your breeder if you decide your Welsh Terrier isn't a good fit with your family. They didn't knowingly send a puppy to an unsuitable home.

I was fortunate that my parents were dog breeders and had a kennel. While I struggled to regain my health and rebuild my life, they took in some of my dogs and found homes for several. Unfortunately, one dog—placed on a trial basis with a verbal agreement the dog would be returned if things didn't work out—was rehomed without permission. The person who had the dog on a trial basis refused to tell my elderly mother where the dog was placed because "it was just too painful to look up the information." I still legally own the dog, and I would love to know where she is and if she is happy or even still alive. Her call name was "Blue." She was born in 2008 and had a microchip registered with HomeAgain. The person who had Blue on a trial basis and placed her without permission lived in North Carolina.

If your breeder can't help, contact WTCARES. This breed-specific rescue understands the breed and will be more helpful than a rescue or shelter lacking Welsh Terrier experience. The people at WTCARES understand that Welshies aren't suitable for every home and that sometimes life circumstances require giving up a beloved pet. You will be treated with respect, and your Welsh terrier will have a good chance of finding an appropriate home.

If you adopted your Welsh Terrier, you are usually contractually obligated to return it to the organization or group that placed it with you if you can no longer keep it. I would also recommend alerting WTCARES about the situation.

CHAPTER 13

Traveling with Your Welsh Terrier

Planning and preparation are the keys to a successful trip with your Welsh Terrier. First, consider your dog's health, comfort, and safety. The best choice for very elderly, sick, or anxious terriers may be not to take them. Also, consider how much time you will have to spend with your Welshie during the trip. Why take your pet if you can't spend a significant amount of time with it?

Photo Courtesy of Steve Ambrosio

Planning Your Trip

Before you travel with your dog, you must do your research. Check and double check airline, train, state, country, and hotel pet policies. You don't want to arrive at the airport and suddenly find out your Welshie can't fly because you don't have all the required documentation for your pet. Or to find out your hotel just changed ownership and no longer accepts dogs.

If you are flying, book direct flights if possible. It's better if your pet doesn't experience layovers, changing planes, and longer travel time. Airlines often limit the number of pets allowed in the cabin and in the baggage hold, so make your reservations early.

There are also temperature restrictions for dogs flying in cargo. When the ground temperature at the departure, layover, or arrival airport is too hot or too cold, dogs can't fly in the baggage hold. Check with your airline about these restrictions.

Sometimes it's a good idea to plan potty breaks for a trip. You should know where your dog is allowed to relieve itself at airports or train stations before you get there. When traveling alone with your dog by car, plan where you yourself will go potty too. You want restrooms that allow your Welshie inside with you because it's never a good idea to leave a dog alone in a parked car. (See more about leaving dogs alone in parked cars at the end of this chapter.) Look for major pet retailers like Petco and PetSmart. Some big stores like Hobby Lobby and Michael's Craft Stores allow dogs inside too.

Download some dog-friendly apps before you go. They can be helpful in planning and useful during the trip. Here are some popular ones:

- *Pet First Aid by American Red Cross* helps you find the closest veterinary emergency clinic. It also provides instructions for basic pet first aid. I consider this a must-have app when traveling with a pet within the United States.
- Both the *Rover* and *Wag!* apps help you find caregivers such as pet sitters and dog walkers around the country.
- The *BringFido* app is a top resource for dog-friendly hotels, restaurants, and attractions around the world.

Dog Crates and Other Restraints

Whether traveling by car, plane, or train, your dog will need some type of restraint to keep it safe. For car travel, there are many options. Domestic airlines and railroad companies, however, have very specific regulations for pets.

For example, there are very strict requirements for airline-compliant pet containers. To learn these specifications, check with individual airlines and the International Air Transport Association (IATA). Each airline has its own regulations for pets flying in cargo and in cabin. However, the minimal container requirements for flying a dog in cargo are usually based on IATA regulations. (https://www.iata.org/en/programs/cargo/live-animals/pets/)

Unfortunately, many adult Welsh Terriers are too large to fly in-cabin on airlines in the United States. Train restrictions also rule out many of these dogs. So, if you plan to take your dog on a train or plane, check out the requirements well ahead of time. Make sure your dog will fit within the required carrier dimensions and weight limit.

Some dog owners accommodate carry-on container restrictions by choosing a taller carrier with a flexible top that compresses to fit the required space. Some small Welsh Terriers can curl up and sleep comfortably inside these carriers while wedged under the seat of a train or plane. Once pulled out from the tight space, the carrier pops back to full height, providing the dog more room. (With this strategy, you risk an airline or train employee refusing to allow the dog to board because it's too big for the carrier when the top flexes down.)

Photo Courtesy of Krystle Sickman

In the car, a Welsh Terrier should always be securely

restrained. A study by Volvo Car USA and the Harris Polls found that dogs riding loose in a car more than doubled unsafe driving behavior and driver distraction caused by the dog. A sudden stop or sharp turn can send an unrestrained dog flying and cause injury. To protect your Welshie and other passengers, restrain it with a secured crate (hard- or soft-sided) or harness during road trips.

> **FUN FACT**
> **Stink-Eye Walk and Social**
>
> Welsh Terriers are infamous for their hallmark stink-eye look, which expresses annoyance and feisty independence. The stink eye is so well known that the Welsh Terrier Rescue (WTCARES) hosts an annual Stink-Eye Walk fundraiser to support their rescue mission. WTCARES was founded in the 1980s and became a charitable trust in 2007. For more information, visit www.welshterrierrescue.com.

Unfortunately, neither the Consumer Products Safety Commission nor the National Highway Traffic Safety Administration provide oversight or regulation for pet containers or seatbelt harnesses. That means they don't verify manufacturers' safety claims for these products. However, the Center for Pet Safety (CPC), a nonprofit research and consumer-advocacy organization founded in 2011, studies pet products to provide unbiased information to pet owners. They crash-test pet crates and safety harnesses. The products that pass their tests are CPC-certified as safe.

You can find a listing of CPC-certified pet containers and travel harnesses on their website (https://www.centerforpetsafety.org). You can also see crash-test videos, including the products that failed. So far, only a few pet travel restraints on the market have been CPC-tested, and even fewer are certified. A few CPC-certified crates are the right size for an adult Welsh Terrier. In addition, CPC-certified safety harnesses come in various sizes, and some should fit your Welshie.

I hope you will check out the CPC website if only to better understand car safety for your dog. You should also be aware that some manufacturers have their pet products independently tested by third-party organizations other than the CPC, and you may have to rely upon them if you can't find a CPC-certified product to meet your needs. Just do your research and make sure a restraint actually passed a real crash

Photo Courtesy of Hayley Rampton

test and that the test was done by a legitimate third-party tester rather than in-house. You can contact a manufacturer for information about their product's crash testing. It might also be helpful to look for product reviews mentioning car accidents while a dog was using the product.

It is very important that your dog's restraint fits properly. The measurements needed to fit a car harness vary from product to product. Some harnesses require a dog's girth size and weight, while others require additional measurements. Follow the individual harness manufacturer's directions for measuring your Welshie to get the correct size.

If you're using a car crate, you will want your dog to fit snugly inside it. There shouldn't be a lot of extra room, or the terrier risks being thrown around inside the container. Your Welshie only needs to curl up and sleep, sit, stand, and turn around. Your dog doesn't have to stretch out completely to be comfortable and safe.

The measurements for a car crate are simple. For the height, measure from the top of your Welshie's shoulders to the ground. Then add three to five inches to this number to calculate the optimal height for the container. For the length, measure from the tip of the nose to the base/root of the tail. For the minimal crate width, measure across the broadest part of your dog (usually the shoulders) and multiply by two.

These numbers will give you an idea of the basic interior dimensions your dog needs.

You must also consider where your dog will ride in the car. Be sure the space is suitable for your choice of restraint. If using a crate, it must be secured so it cannot slide or shift because of an abrupt stop.

A Welshie should ride in the back seat or cargo area of a car. In the cargo area, make sure your dog is NOT riding within the car's crumple zone. (This area crumples and absorbs energy in a crash.) Your Welsh Terrier should also not ride in the front seat because the airbag could injure or kill it.

Whatever your mode of transportation, a crate, hard-sided or soft-sided, will also need bedding. It should be comfortable for your dog to lie on for long periods of time. You'll probably want to include several layers of absorbent material (like pee pads) for airline flights.

Preparing Your Welsh Terrier for the Trip

Once you have a travel crate or harness, acclimate your Welsh Terrier to it. Don't take your dog on a trip without first getting it used to its safety restraint. Whatever the mode of transportation, your dog needs to learn to be relaxed and comfortable for extended periods in its safety restraint. There will be lots of people and noise on train and plane trips, so introduce these factors to your crated dog prior to traveling.

Sedation of pets for air travel is not recommended by the American Veterinary Medical Association. In fact, some airlines do not allow sedated pets to fly.

If your Welsh Terrier is an anxious traveler, behavior modification can ease that anxiety. Start with short local trips accompanied by lots of positive reinforcement, and gradually make the trips longer. A terrier can also get used to staying in its travel crate at home. Start with a short time in the crate and gradually extend it. Make the crate into a happy place where the dog enjoys its favorite chew toy. Your Welshie can learn to relax in its carrier or harness on a trip with your help.

Teach your terrier to wait for a command to leave its carrier when the door opens. You should be able to reach into the container and attach

Photo Courtesy of Lisa Tucker

the leash to your Welshie before it tries to exit. Only after you give a command to exit should your dog leave the crate. This trained behavior could save your Welsh Terrier's life when traveling.

Make sure your pet's vaccinations, ID, and license tags are up to date. For airline travel, a dog will need proof of vaccination and other health documents. Check with your airline to find out exactly what you need. If you are flying internationally, research the requirements of any countries you are traveling to and what you need to return home. Then work with your veterinarian to make sure your dog meets all the health requirements.

Your Welsh Terrier should be microchipped in addition to having its collar ID and tags for any trip. If you are using a crate, your contact information and destination information should be readily available on the container. It is always a good idea to place a "Live Animal" label on a crate. (This label is required for air travel in cargo.) It is also a good idea to attach a current photo of your dog to its carrier. (You should also carry a current photo of your terrier on your phone or print it out in case the dog gets loose.)

Dangling tags on your Welsh Terrier's collar might catch on crate doors or vents and lead to strangulation. I know someone who tapes her dog's dangling tags flat against its collar when it travels. I myself prefer a dog-tag pocket/pouch that lies flat when attached to the collar, like the Ruthi Tag Tote. A breakaway collar also prevents strangulation from caught tags, but you must be careful when attaching the leash. If the leash isn't attached to both D-rings, this type of collar will break away because of pressure from the leash.

Chapter 13: Traveling with Your Welsh Terrier

Packing for Your Dog

>
>
> *Welsh Terriers make great travel companions! They are usually up for anything, and adventures are always welcome. I would travel with a crate and make sure to pack the dog's 'suitcase' as well as your own. This would include an extra collar and lead, bedding, dishes, toys, and food and treats.*
>
> **EMILY CARROLL**
> *Bayleigh Carroway Welsh Terriers*
>
>

When I travel with my Welsh Terrier, some of the items I like to pack include:

- Extra leash and collar/harness
- Medications and nutritional supplements
- Flea and tick preventative
- Pet first aid kit
- Food
  - It is never a good idea to change food when traveling. If your dog's regular food is not readily available at your travel destination, pack enough for the trip plus enough extra to last several days.
- Treats
- Brushes and comb (nail clipper/grinder for extended trips)
- Several of my dog's favorite toys, including a chew toy
- Poop bags
- Cleaning supplies for any accidents
- Extra bedding for the crate
- A towel
- Extra copies of my dog's travel documents
- Copies of my dog's medical records in case of veterinary emergency
- Collapsible food and water dishes
- Plenty of bottled water for car trips

Photo Courtesy of Bonnie Hall

Travel Tips

The day prior to travel, make sure your Welshie gets plenty of exercise. A high-energy dog may travel better if it uses up some energy the day before the trip. On the day of your journey, remember to take your terrier for a short potty walk before departure.

It's a good idea to feed your Welsh Terrier less on the day of a long journey, and don't give it food right before you leave. Instead, feed your dog a light meal at least four hours before leaving home. Continue to offer water. Stopping food four hours before traveling helps avoid an upset tummy during the trip. If you must feed your terrier while traveling in a car, stop and let the dog eat, drink water, and go potty before continuing your trip.

It is never a good idea to leave a dog alone in a parked car. In hot weather, even parked in the shade with the windows cracked, a car can reach dangerous temperatures in minutes and cause canine heatstroke. Cars get dangerously hot when parked in the sun during mild weather too. Some people leave a dog in the car with the air conditioner running, but ACs can malfunction and cars can stall. In cold weather, a vehicle can become too cold, causing a dog to develop hypothermia. Leaving your dog unattended in an automobile may also expose it to pet theft.

If you must leave your Welshie alone in the car, make it quick and use your common sense to keep your terrier safe. Windshield sunshades as well as AC may help in some situations, as will parking where you can see the car from inside the building. Above all, don't dawdle when your dog is alone in the car, and don't leave it alone at all if the situation can be avoided.

When you arrive at your destination, make sure your room or house is puppy-proof before your dog is released inside. Don't assume a hotel or B&B will be completely clean and safe for your dog just because of the cleaning staff. If visiting family, it's still a good idea to check for any potential dog hazards.

Try to maintain a regular schedule for feeding and walking your Welsh Terrier while away from home. This will help your dog adjust to the new environment.

If you must leave your terrier alone in a hotel room, make sure it is in a crate. Provide a chew toy, such as a Kong stuffed with a little peanut butter, to keep the pup occupied while you are out. I like to leave the television turned on to a sitcom channel so my dog can hear the steady chatter of voices while I'm out. I also leave the Do Not Disturb sign on the door, and I try not to stay out too long. If your Welshie will be alone for many hours, consider hiring a pet sitter.

Clean up any mess your pet creates in the hotel room immediately. Don't leave it for the cleaning staff. Keep your Welshie on a leash while roaming the hotel grounds and common areas. Remember that not every stranger you see will want to meet your dog.

If a hotel has a designated potty area for dogs, use it and clean up after your terrier. Nobody, not even other dog owners, likes an owner that doesn't pick up after their pet. It makes all dog owners look bad. Hotels that have unpleasant experiences with canine guests may consider banning all dogs in the future.

When You Can't Take Your Dog on a Trip

If your Welsh Terrier can't travel with you, make arrangements for its care well before your departure date. A family member or trusted friend that the dog already knows may be able to care for it. If that is not an option, do your research and find a good pet sitter or boarding kennel for your Welsh Terrier. The difference between the two is that your dog will get to stay in your home with a pet sitter, while a kennel is a sort of dog hotel that cares for your pet in a safe environment. Some pet sitters will board your Welshie in their home, so it's still in a home environment, just not yours.

These services tend to book well in advance, so don't wait till the last minute to make a reservation for your dog. Ask dog-owning friends and family, as well as your veterinarian, trainer, and groomer, for recommendations. Websites such as Rover (www.rover.com) and Wag! (www.wagwalking.com) also provide information about pet sitters and kennels nationwide. Once you have some possibilities, look at their online reviews to help narrow down your list.

In your initial contact with a pet sitter or boarding kennel, you want to find out if they are bonded and insured. What licenses or certifications do they have? Every state has different regulations for these businesses, and not all states require pet sitters to be licensed.

Ask what training the staff has. You also want to know about backup personnel for a pet sitter in case the primary person becomes incapacitated. Training will vary, but all staff should at least be trained in dog first aid. Ask about their procedures for emergencies too.

If you are considering a kennel or boarding at a pet sitter's home, ask whether all dogs are required to be up to date on vaccinations. Also, find out about the daily routine, how often your terrier will be fed, and how much exercise it will get.

At a kennel, you may want to pay extra for your Welshie to have individual playtime with a staff member or a solo walk. It's worth it for a breed that craves that human connection. I would not recommend having your Welsh Terrier exercise in a playgroup at a boarding facility. Also, find out if a kennel is heated or air-conditioned.

Ask for a tour of a boarding site. If you can't see where your dog will be staying, you don't want it to stay there. You want to check how clean and secure it is. Think about your terrier's individual personality and whether it would be comfortable in the environment you observe.

If you are hiring an in-home pet sitter, you want to slowly introduce them to your dog before you leave. Have them meet the pet in your home, take your dog for several walks, and do at least one mini-in-home visit that includes feeding your pet prior to your departure.

Whether you choose a pet sitter or a kennel, you want a knowledgeable staff that likes dogs and works with them in a positive manner in an environment where your dog will be safe and comfortable.

CHAPTER 14

Activities for Welsh Terriers

> *Welsh Terriers are intelligent, and if they do not get adequate physical and mental exercise, they can become destructive as they look for ways to entertain themselves. The saying 'A tired dog is a good dog' does have some truth to it! Walking the dog (with time allowed for sniffing), engaging in play with the family, and playing with a dog friend are all good mental and physical activities. Interactive toys and puzzles, snuffle mats, and training games or classes are also good mental stimulation.*
>
> JUDITH FORD ANSPACH
> *Abbeyrose Welsh Terriers*

When you think about a fun activity for your Welsh Terrier, a walk around town or a game of fetch in the yard may come to mind. Or perhaps you think of cuddling with your lapdog. But if you want to try something different, there is an entire world of organized dog sports and activities that your Welshie might enjoy.

Channeling your terrier's zest for life into one of these activities can help you build a stronger bond as well as provide mental and physical exercise for a Welshie. These pursuits also help train and socialize your dog.

One of the best places to sample some of these activities is at informal fun events put on by dog clubs, 4-H clubs, rescue groups, and training centers. These events go by different names, but they are basically doggy fun days that offer introductions to a variety of activities like agility, Earthdog, rally, nose work, barn hunt, and trick dog. Canine Good Citizen (CGC) testing is sometimes available too.

For a small fee, you and your dog can get an introductory taste of an activity with guidance from an experienced dog person. There are usually multiple activities to sample, and you can try as many as you and your Welshie desire.

I especially enjoy fun days hosted by terrier clubs. Some of the regional Welsh Terrier Clubs, such as the Welsh Terrier Club of Southern California and the Welsh Terrier Club of Northern Illinois, have events like this. The Glyndwr Welsh Terrier Club in the Northeast has held a variety of social and educational events for Welsh Terriers and their owners for decades.

It's always fun to meet and socialize with other terrier aficionados. Some regional Welsh Terrier clubs host fun walks where you can meet and socialize with other owners. The Stinkeye walk/party for Welshies is held in a different city every year with the proceeds benefiting WTCARES. You can contact the rescue group for more information about this event.

Faux Hunting Games

> *Welsh Terriers excel in all performance events. Depending on their prey drive, they may be better at finding rats in Earth Dog and Barn Hunt, or may be more pack animals who excel in Obedience, Rally, and Freestyle. Sometimes they just like to run a lure course or Fast Cat—who doesn't like to chase moving objects, right? Some Welshies are better at different things, but they all have special talents that the owner needs to discover to help the dog live its best life.*
>
> ANNE PELLETIER
> *Bremadog Welsh*

Photo Courtesy of John Melair

Simulated go-to-ground and ratting tests may be the most fun a Welsh Terrier can have without hunting. This breed was created to hunt vermin below and above ground, and it still possesses the instincts for that job. Den trials and ratting tests allow owners to work with their dogs' natural drives instead of against them. Even though these are just games rather than actual hunts, the activities help owners better understand a Welshie's working instinct and let the dogs scratch that inborn itch.

Other than after an actual hunt, I think Welsh Terriers appear happier and prouder following a go-to-ground test than any other activity. I have seen Welshies literally prancing about joyfully after finishing a den trial run.

Go-to-ground tests consist of a man-made tunnel system that a dog traverses to reach quarry (rats) at the end. The tunnel is scented so a dog can follow the smell to its quarry, which is always well protected from the dog. Once a dog reaches the rats, it must work (scratch, dig, or bark) the quarry for a certain amount of time. The tunnel system increases in length and complexity as the test level advances.

There are two primary organizations offering go-to-ground trials in the United States: The American Working Terrier Association (AWTA) and the American Kennel Club (AKC). A dog earns titles or certificates by qualifying in den trials sanctioned by one of these two outfits.

Chapter 14: Activities for Welsh Terriers

The AWTA (www.awta.org) was formed in 1971 by Patricia Lent to encourage the use of Earthdog breeds for hunting both above and below ground. From the beginning, this organization sought to educate people about the correct qualities (character, size, and conformation) necessary for a working terrier.

The first AWTA den trial was held in June 1971. Mrs. Lent saw artificial den trials as an educational event for owners where dogs could use their hunting instincts and their owners could socialize with people experienced in hunting terriers and dachshunds. All AWTA den trial judges are experienced with hunting dogs in the earth.

The AWTA also awards certificates to dogs for actual hunting. A Working Certificate is awarded to a dog for working specific wild quarry below ground in a natural den. A Hunting Certificate is awarded for hunting specific quarry above ground. If you want to learn more about terriers going-to-ground and hunting for real, joining the AWTA is a good place to start.

Only one Welshie has ever earned an AWTA Working Certificate. Welsh Terrier bitch Welsh Pac's Royal Promise CDX, CG, WC, owned by Diane Amendola, earned her WC entering a natural den and working a raccoon. Amendola was out hunting with Teddy Moritz (whom many consider a guru of American Earthdog hunting) on the day her terrier earned a WC in October 1987. This dog was in a natural tunnel alongside another Welsh Terrier (also belonging to Amendola) and a Dachshund working a raccoon for forty-five minutes. Amendola is a den trial judge for both AWTA and AKC, so ask her about hunting with Welshies if you are lucky enough to meet her at an event.

The first Earthdog trial licensed by the AKC was held in Oregon in October 1994. These trials are now offered nationwide and have grown in popularity since their introduction. The AKC has four test levels: Intro, Junior, Senior, and Master. The AKC awards titles to dogs at each level for qualifying a certain number of times. Recently, the AKC added an Endurance Earthdog title for dogs that pass both the Senior and Master Level tests on the same day.

For the Intro, Junior, and Senior tests, the dogs run individually. At the end of the Senior test, the rats are removed from the tunnel, and the handler recalls the dog. I want to advise against trying to tackle your dog to complete the recall at the end of the Senior test. If time runs out before you catch your dog, it is not the end of the world. I see nothing good about a grown person throwing themselves onto a dog in order to catch it and get a qualifying score. A dog isn't likely to run away from the Earthdog site. The many good smells and other dogs and friendly people will entice it to stay in the vicinity.

The problem is that when the rats are removed from the Senior tunnel and you call your terrier, it often emerges in hunting mode. It is still looking for prey. If your dog pops out of the tunnel entrance near you, you can easily pick it up. If your dog pops out of a tunnel opening further away, the recall can be a little tricky. If you run toward a Welshie to catch it, the dog may turn and run away from you. I think these dogs believe you have spotted prey, and they are moving in the direction you indicate with your own movement.

There is a simple way to recall a dog that is still focused on hunting. Make the dog think there is prey near you. Indicate interest in the area beside you—maybe even shaking the grass as you call your Welshie—and the dog should come to investigate. That is a much better strategy to quickly catch your terrier than tackling it.

My husband once tried to tackle a sweet little Welsh Terrier for the Senior Earthdog recall. Fortunately, he missed. But our Welshie was traumatized by the attempt and, afterwards, was afraid to come out of an Earthdog tunnel when called.

Welsh Terrier owner John Melair is an excellent example of the attitude required to enjoy life with a terrier. He missed catching his Welshie Jeb in a Senior Earthdog test but didn't try to tackle the dog to get a qualifying score. Melair and his terrier had a fun day in the country without qualifying. Someone took a picture of Jeb running past his owner during the Senior recall, and Melair made that his cover picture on Facebook. You could see the joy on Jeb's face in that photo. Even when life doesn't go as planned with Welsh Terriers, it can still be enjoyed.

In the Master level test, the dogs run in pairs, and the pairs are randomly drawn from the class entrants. After the dogs locate the Master tunnel, the dogs enter it one at a time to work the rats. The dog outside the tunnel must be quiet and honor the dog working in the tunnel. This behavior is patterned off the conduct of Earthdogs on real hunts. Hunters need to hear what is happening inside the earth when a dog is working quarry, and they won't tolerate a dog standing above the earth barking.

In my experience, most Welsh Terriers do not need special training for the beginning den test of either organization. The typical Welsh Terrier will follow its nose into the tunnel and find the rats with no prior experience. Novice dogs usually crawl cautiously and slowly the first time they enter an artificial den. They often fail to reach the rats in time to qualify on the initial run. However, that first experience is usually all it takes for most Welshies to understand the game and fly through the tunnel the next chance they get.

When my husband and I packed the car and headed to our first den trial with Bear, we didn't know what to expect. After listening to the orientation, the two of us watched other participants with their dogs. Then it was my turn to run Bear in the novice class. Walking to the release point where I would turn him loose, I was nervous. Earthdog expert JoAnn Frier-Murza had assured me that my dog would do what came naturally and follow the scent to the tunnel, and I hoped she was right. My dog wasn't trained to do this.

I pointed to the tunnel opening, told Bear to "go get 'em," and let him loose to follow his nose. Bear tracked the scent to the entrance of the tunnel and sniffed around before deciding to enter slowly. He must have crawled cautiously through the darkness, because it seemed like an eternity before I heard him bark at the rats at the end.

After Bear barked for a short time, the judge called me over to the tunnel's end and lifted the top so I could see Bear. I patted him for a minute and told him what a good boy he was. Then it was time to lift my dog out of the tunnel.

He failed the test that day because he was too slow, but he was happy and extremely proud of himself. The next time we went to a den trial, Bear easily earned a qualifying score because he remembered the game.

I have seen a few terriers (never a Welsh) who were great workers in a natural earth on a real hunt but who refused to play any faux hunting games. So, it is possible for a terrier with a working instinct to turn its nose up at these den games. If that happens with your dog, don't despair; just find another activity to enjoy with your dog. Also, if your dog is great at den trials, don't assume it will be a great worker hunting for real in a natural earth. The only way to know if a dog is an excellent hunter is to hunt it.

There are two organizations offering above-ground ratting tests for dogs in the United States—the Barn Hunt Association and the North American Sporting Dog Association (NASDA). Both require participants to register their dogs with the organization to take part in events. Most dogs do not require any type of special training to enter the beginning level tests of either organization.

The Barn Hunt Association (www.barnhunt.com) offers a variety of tests where rats in PVC tubes are hidden throughout a course constructed of hay bales. Empty tubes and tubes with soiled rat bedding are also hidden on the course. A dog must find the rats, go through the tunnel, and jump on the hay bale within the allotted time to pass the test. The handler must be able to read their dog to know when it has found a rat. A certain number of passes are required to title and move on to the next level. The difficulty of the tests increases with each level. The AKC recognizes titles earned with the Barn Hunt Association.

The NASDA (https://nasda.dog) offers two different tests for locating rats. Trailing and Locating is a test that requires a dog to follow a scent out in the open to find a rat hidden in a protective quarry box. In the Urban Locating test, simulating ratting in an urban environment, a dog locates a rat without a scent trail in an urban environment, such as a warehouse, barn, developed garden, or shed. Once again, the rat is hidden in a protective quarry box. Dogs can earn qualifying points in a test, and when they have accumulated enough points, they earn a title. Both tests have different levels that increase in difficulty as the dog advances.

Few modern Welsh Terriers get to hunt below or above ground, but the breed still retains its working instincts. Max Searls's bear-hunting Welshie Roy was proof of that. According to Searls, Roy was his best buddy. Together they hunted bears and enjoyed many outdoor adventures. Searls's Welshie was great with his kids, got along with other dogs, and was an incredibly loyal companion for almost 13 years. Sounds like a dog that was happy in his work and his life. I hope that some of my readers will at least give their Welsh Terriers a chance to revel in their working instinct at some of the faux hunt games. In my experience, these activities can make your dog a lot happier.

Chapter 14: Activities for Welsh Terriers

The author with her dog Bear in parade of champions

Starting Your Welsh Terrier in Fieldwork

by Diane Amendola

(Learn the quarry in the area and any dangers associated with them before you start.)

1. Walk your dog where there are burrows. When your dog shows an interest, tell him "good dog." If you don't want the dog to work the hole, just calmly say "leave it" and walk him away. Always do this activity on leash so you can control it.
2. If your dog shows no interest, walk on; there is probably no creature home. Trust your dog!
3. When your dog becomes excited and begins to dig, pat him (do not pet him; petting is for soothing—patting is for exciting him) saying, "Good dog." This helps form a working relationship with your dog, getting him to accept you as his partner. Good dogs never hide or threaten the handler (aggressively growling or snarling) when being removed from working.
4. When you've had enough, close the hole as best you can, repairing what the dog did.

Setting up the Master Earth for an AKC

Young Welsh Terrier being introduced to rats

Chapter 14: Activities for Welsh Terriers

Welsh Terrier entering earthdog tunnel

Sue Weiss introducing her Welsh Terrier puppy

Bear enters an earthdog tunnel at high speed

Welsh Terrier at the end of an earthdog tunnel

Welsh Terrier being removed

Companion Activities

The AKC's Canine Good Citizen (CGC) program, rally obedience, competitive obedience, trick dog, dancing with your dog, and therapy dog certification are all activities that improve your connection to your dog through training. Earning a CGC certificate shows your Welsh Terrier has the good manners necessary both at home and in public. Dogs must pass a 10-skill test that includes things like walking on a loose lead, sitting and staying on command, and coming when called. These tests are performed in a ring with simulations of real-world occurrences, such as a crowd of people.

There are many obedience classes around the country designed to help dog-owner teams master the required skills for this test. It is not a competitive sport, but mastering the skills enriches your relationship with your Welshie. It also provides a good foundation of training for other canine sports, such as obedience and agility.

After your dog earns its CGC, there are two more advanced certificates to work toward: the AKC Community Canine and the AKC Urban CGC. Both programs have a 10-skill test. The Community Canine test is performed in real-life situations, such as a dog show or a busy sidewalk. The Urban CGC test focuses on skills needed by dogs living in a city and is administered in settings with the smells and noises of a city, traffic, and crowds. Dogs must have earned an AKC CGC to be eligible to test for one of these advanced certificates.

If you live on a farm or just want to try something different with your Welsh Terrier, you might try the AKC Farm Dog Certified Test. A dog performs 12 exercises related to farm life in this test, such as being under control and calm near livestock and jumping on a hay bale and staying.

HISTORICAL FACT

Best in Show

A Welsh Terrier has taken home the Best in Show title at the annual Westminster Kennel Club Dog Show only once since the club's inaugural show in 1907. This lucky champion was named Ch. Flornell-Rare-Bit of Twin Ponds, and won the Best in Show title in 1944.

If you love those quiet moments in training when your dog figures out what you want, you might enjoy competitive obedience—rally or traditional or both. It requires a lot of training, and there will be many of those light-bulb moments with your Welshie. The most important thing in this sport is finding an instructor who makes training fun for you and your terrier and doesn't think terriers are hard to train. Look for a teacher whose dogs are happy workers and whose students' dogs are just as happy.

Rally obedience is a newer and more relaxed form of competitive obedience based on traditional obedience. In this sport, a judge sets out a course of signs which each list a skill for a dog and handler to perform. The teams heel individually through the course, performing the required skill at each sign. Handlers can praise and interact with their dogs throughout the course. Since every course is unique, you won't get bored with repeating the same old pattern of exercises in competition. You work your way through the course continuously. Rally is more fun and less rigid than traditional obedience competitions.

Some people find formal obedience to be rigid and monotonous, but I enjoyed the stability of knowing the same exercises would always be repeated in the same order in competition. (You don't have to practice the exercises in the same pattern every day.) In traditional obedience competition, the exercises are slightly broken up by the judge, allowing you to regroup a little in between. I get very nervous in competition, so it was nice to have these mini breaks.

Focused attention training is important for success in both rally and traditional obedience. This work forges a stronger bond between you and your dog, whichever type of obedience you try. Just remember that Welsh Terriers learn best with positive reinforcement methods. Then, when you think you are ready for the competition ring, give it a test run in some informal fun matches first. Several organizations sanction competitions and offer titles in rally obedience and formal obedience, including the AKC.

For people who like teaching their dog tricks, there are organizations that offer titles to trick dogs. I think trick training is a wonderful way to build a stronger bond with a Welsh Terrier. Plus, you get to show off your Welshie's superior intelligence while impressing friends and family with

Chapter 14: Activities for Welsh Terriers

Photo Courtesy of Max Searls

Ashley Searls - Age 12 - with bear she harvested with Roy

Photo Courtesy of Max Searls

Roy

Roy the Bear Hunter

"My Welsh Terrier Roy was an amazing companion to the point of being jealous of other dogs and people, including my wife. If I didn't take him hunting, it was her fault in his mind and he would pee on her craft projects, or even her pillow a couple of times. But he liked her too—just not the same. If strangers came to visit, he would use his own judgement sometimes let them pet him, but other times he would piss in their shoes, and for a few he would stay between us in an almost aggressive manner. He was a one of a kind—the best buddy I ever had."

-Max Searls, Hunting Guide/Outfitter in the Cariboo Region of British Columbia, Canada, on his dog Roy (a registered Welsh Terrier used to recover and stop wounded bears until the hunter can dispatch them)

Photo Courtesy of Linda Brisbin

performances. Two groups that offer trick titles are the AKC and Do More With Your Dog (https://domorewithyourdog.com/DogTricks/). There are advancing levels of trick dog titles. To earn a title, your dog must perform a certain number of tricks prescribed for the level. If you've already taught your Welsh Terrier some tricks, it may be able to earn a trick dog title already. I have a friend who happened upon a trick dog event in a park, tried it with her dog, and earned a novice trick dog title.

Have you ever considered dancing with your Welsh Terrier? It is a canine sport that involves obedience, tricks, and sometimes a little agility choreographed to music. There are fabulous dog dancing routines posted on YouTube. One of my favorite videos is a Charlie Chaplin–based dog dance.

The three major organizations offering titles in dog dancing are:

- World Canine Freestyle Organization (https://www.worldcaninefreestyle.org)
- Canine Freestyle Federation Inc. (https://canine-freestyle.org)
- Musical Dog Sport Associations (https://musicaldogsport.org)

Chapter 14: Activities for Welsh Terriers

Some Welsh Terriers and their owners take part in this sport in the United States and around the world. It looks like great fun for anyone with a good sense of rhythm and the ability to make training fun for a dog.

Do you think your Welsh Terrier is a good therapist? Those happy tail wags, attention, and tricks can bring a smile to anyone's face. You could take your terrier's therapy work on the road with visits to facilities such as nursing homes, hospices, and libraries. First, you need to get your dog certified with a therapy dog organization. There are quite a few. The oldest is Therapy Dogs International (TDI), formed in 1976. TDI (https://www.tdi-dog.org) is a volunteer organization that tests, certifies, registers, and insures therapy dogs and their handlers. Volunteering with a certified therapy dog can enrich your life as you and your terrier bring joy to others.

Bear learning the agility dog walk obstacle

Welsh Terrier puppy learning the agility tunnel.

Speedy Dog Sports

Welsh Terriers usually enjoy showing off their capacity for speed. While not a hyperactive breed, they are thrilled with fast-paced canine sports. I am always amazed that my Welshies enjoy activities with a slow-moving, uncoordinated human like me. Fortunately, there are some speedy sports we can enjoy with our dogs, and a couple of them don't require a human handler to be fast.

CAT (Coursing Ability Test) and FastCAT are AKC events open to all breeds based on the sport of lure coursing. These are timed events where dogs run individually over a course, chasing a lure made of plastic strips. Years before the AKC sanctioned these events for all breeds, I tried lure coursing with my Welshies at a terrier fun day. They loved it.

CAT is a pass/fail event that allows dogs to earn titles based on the number of times they have earned a passing score. Dogs measuring less than 12 inches at the withers run a 300-yard course in less than 90 seconds to pass. Dogs taller than 12 inches run a 600-yard course in under two minutes to pass. (Owners may choose to run only two-thirds of a course with a veteran dog.)

Chapter 14: Activities for Welsh Terriers

Fast CAT is more of a lure coursing sprint. It is a 100-yard dash where dogs individually chase a lure. The dog's time is converted to MPH (miles per hour) and then multiplied by a handicap based on the dog's height to determine the number of points the dog earned. The AKC awards Fast CAT titles to dogs based on their accumulation of points.

The Jack Russell Terrier Club of America (JRTCA) sanctions terrier races for Jack Russell Terriers. Some JRTCA events offer nonsanctioned classes for other terrier breeds. There are two types of JRTCA terrier races: flat and steeplechase. Dogs (usually wearing soft muzzles) are place into a starting box, like a starting gate for horse races. When the box opens, the dogs chase a scented lure down the course (over small jumps in steeplechase races) to stacked haybales at the end with a hole in the middle. The lure is pulled through the hole in the hay, and the dogs chase it. The first dog over the finish line on the other side of the bales wins that race heat. You can find information about upcoming events on the JRTCA website (https://www.therealjackrussell.com).

Flyball is a relay race event for dogs and their humans. Teams consist of four dogs and handlers. Dogs race individually over a course of four jumps to a box with a tennis ball. When a dog pounces on the angled pad of this box, it launches a tennis ball that the dog retrieves/catches. Then the dog (with ball in mouth) races over the jumps back to the start/finish line. As soon as a dog crosses the finish line, the next dog can start the course.

Jump height is based on the size of the smallest dog on the team. Two teams each race side by side over a 51-foot course. The first team to have all four dogs finish the course wins.

The two major organizations sanctioning flyball events and awarding titles are the North American Flyball Association (NAFA, http://www.flyball.org) and the United Flyball League International (https://www.u-fli.com). The AKC recognizes titles earned with the NAFA. You can contact these two leagues to locate a flyball club in your area offering classes.

Agility may be the most well-known dog sport. In agility, dogs race over a course of jumps, weave poles, tunnels, and other obstacles at the direction of their handler. It is a great way to have fun with a terrier and keep you and the dog in shape. In my experience, many Welsh Terriers love this sport. Even though handlers have to traverse the course, too, you can train a terrier to be handled from a distance, so you don't have to run as fast as your dog.

There are many organizations that sanction agility events and offer titles. Three popular venues are:

- United States Dog Agility Association Inc (USDAA, https://www.usdaa.com)
- North American Dog Agility Council (NADAC, https://www.nadac.com)
- American Kennel Club (AKC, https://www.akc.org)

Quite a few Welsh Terriers have enjoyed success in agility in the United States. Linda Brisbin's dog Webster (MACH14 ADCH Cisseldale's Double Trouble RE MXS4 MJC4 JE) achieved a few agility firsts for the breed. In 1999, he was the first Welsh Terrier to earn an Agility Dog Championship in the USDAA. Webster made history again in 2002, becoming the first Welsh Terrier to earn an AKC Master Agility Championship. In 2020, Linda Brisbin's dog Patrick (AGCH MACH5 WYSIWYG Trouble Has Arrived MXC2 PDG MJC2 PJG MFG TWX) became the first Welsh Terrier AKC Agility Grand Champion.

> *Training a Welsh Terrier in agility is one of the biggest joys of my life. My experience is that Welshies need a job, or they'll create one of their own, and it may not be what you want.*
>
> *Watching an independent contractor choose to surrender the lead and trust I'll only provide fun and games is heartwarming.*
>
> *I've trained 5 Welsh Terriers for agility, and all became agility champions, from the First AKC Champion to the First AKC Grand Champion.*
>
> *They love being correct. Train to their strong points. Don't over-train with repetitions, as they will become bored and offer alternatives to your goal. Change things up and reward, reward, reward!!!*
>
> *They are brilliant dogs, all with different personalities and learn at their own pace.*
>
> *Bring a sense of humor and patience, and you and your Welsh Terrier will be rewarded beyond your dreams in this addictive sport.*
>
> *See you at the finish line,*
> *Linda Brisbin*

Chapter 14: Activities for Welsh Terriers

Photo Courtesy of Annie McAnespie

While there aren't many breeds as fast and capable in agilty as Welsh Terriers, Welshies do require a lot of consistent training to succeed. If you keep at it, all that time and effort can pay off. At the 1999 FCI World Agility Championships in Germany, a Welsh Terrier from Finland named Dirty Harry (FI CH C.I.A. FI & SE & NO AgCh Vicway Dirty Harry) won the gold medal in the Mini division.

My trainer Diane Bauman with her American Cocker Spaniel was at the 1999 FCI World Championships as a member of the AKC/USA Agility team and watched the Welsh Terrier's gold medal winning performances in person. According to Bauman, "Dirty Harry was nothing short of a speeding bullet. Agility is a very natural sport for a dog, and watching him was like watching a terrier on the hunt."

As the popularity of this sport has grown, the number of agility trainers has skyrocketed. Be careful when choosing an agility trainer. Look for an instructor who has not only put advanced agility titles on multiple dogs (preferably of different breeds) of their own but also has taught students (with various breeds) who have earned advanced agility titles. Of course, you should always look for a teacher that uses positive training methods and doesn't think terriers are hard to train.

> *When it comes to the Welsh Terrier, agility is the best thing you and your dog can think of. I have bred, trained, and competed several dogs to their agility championships, so I have felt the magic of seamless cooperation, deep frustration, and the joy of discovery.*
>
> *First of all, you need to build super-strong motivation in your dog. Some will find their inner "obstacle hunter" in the very first training session. Most need more time to find it. Welshies are smart but always remember never to give your dog a chance to follow its own protocol while waiting in place or performing contacts. If you give them a chance to slip just a little bit, they won't forget, and it will grow into a big problem. Always keep this in mind and be very precise.*
>
> *The most important thing is to enjoy your training and—possibly—competing. There is never a dull moment, and you simply can't take it too seriously if your dog is independent and clever, as our Welshie friends tend to be. Keep a twinkle in your eye, and let your Welsh Terrier enjoy its work! They love it! Have a nice time with this very addictive sport!*
>
> Sari Mäkelä
> (Breeder of the Finnish Welsh Terrier FI CH C.I.A. FI & SE & NO AgCh Vicway Dirty Harry, 1999 FCI World Agility Champion)

Finnish Welsh Terrier, 1999 FCI Agility World Champion

The Nose Knows

Dogs have an amazing sense of smell, and there are a variety of events to test your Welsh Terrier's nose. The AKC sanctions events and offers titles in both Scent Work and Tracking. Dogs can also compete in the National Association of Canine Scent Work (NACSW) trials for titles. A few Welsh Terriers have been certified for Search and Rescue, and in Europe, some Welshies have been certified in Blood Tracking. Nose work can provide both mental stimulation and physical exercise for a Welsh Terrier.

Have Fun and Make Friends as Your Dog Earns Accolades

My dog Bear and I made many new friends and had a blast exploring different canine disciplines. Along the way, he earned numerous performance titles, became a certified therapy dog, and was recognized as a WTCA Versatility Supreme Champion. By the end of our fun-filled journey together, this conformation champion had become Ch. Rubicon's Sugar Bear, CD, OA, OAJ, NJP, ME, CG, CGC.

CHAPTER 15

The Senior Welsh Terrier

The average life span for Welsh Terriers is 12 to 15 years; however, dogs enjoying life at ages beyond that are not unheard of. I've been fortunate to have some Welshies that relished life until 17, 18, and 19 years of age.

Every dog ages differently. Many Welshies develop arthritis to varying degrees in their old age. Some may experience hearing loss and diminished vision. Old dogs can also develop a type of dementia called canine cognitive dysfunction.

Basics of Senior Dog Care

Much depends on an individual dog's genetics, but there are ways you can help your senior dog maintain good health for as long as possible.

- Adjust your terrier's diet. A dog's dietary needs change as it passes through different life stages. Based on your senior Welshie's blood work, along with any physical or cognitive health issues, you may need to adjust its diet. (Prescription diets are available for dogs with certain conditions, such as kidney or heart problems.) Also, feeding several small meals a day may work better for a senior dog than one enormous meal.
- Ask your vet about supplements, probiotics, and medication that may help your senior canine's issues.
- Monitor water intake. You want to make sure a senior terrier is staying well hydrated. If you think your dog isn't drinking enough, you

Photo Courtesy of Hayley Rampton

can add water to its food to help with hydration. Rather than just one water bowl, you can place a water bowl near all your dog's favorite places to help it remember to drink. An old dog that suddenly starts drinking more water than usual could be developing a health problem. So, consult your veterinarian unless it's a hot day, or the dog is more active than usual.

- Get veterinary check-ups and blood work. Your senior Welshie should have wellness checks once or twice a year. It's also a good idea to do annual blood work. This will show how well your pet's kidneys and liver are functioning and help catch health problems early.
- Discuss vaccinations with your vet and ask about an antibody blood test (titer test). This blood analysis will show whether previous vaccinations are still protecting your dog from some diseases.
- Adapt exercise according to your senior Welshie's needs. As your terrier ages, it may require shorter, more frequent walks rather than a few long walks each day. Swimming is a great exercise for a senior dog because it's low impact and easy on arthritic joints. Whatever exercise you choose, be aware of your pet's needs so you can make an activity easier when necessary.

- Mental stimulation helps protect against cognitive decline. Dog puzzles, snuffle mats, treat-dispensing balls, and nosework/scentwork games provide both mental and physical exercise. Even an elderly Welshie with poor eyesight and hearing can enjoy this fun.
- Keep your senior pet's toenails trimmed. Long nails can cause pain and make it more difficult for a senior dog to walk.
- Dental problems can affect your older Welsh Terrier's ability to eat, so keep brushing its teeth as it ages. Similar to people, dogs get gum disease, and this can spread to other parts of their body. If needed, your vet may recommend a professional dental cleaning. Should your pet have trouble chewing, you can provide wet or soft food that is easy to ingest.

Helping Your Dog Adapt to Old Age

> *Welshies are very active into their senior years, barring any medical issues that may cause problems. Keep them active, but don't overdo, and keep an eye out for any arthritis issues that senior dogs sometimes develop. Terriers in general have a higher-than-average pain threshold; by the time they start to show signs of discomfort, they may already be in a lot of pain, so observe your Welshie carefully over the years. Regular vet examinations will help as well.*
>
> ELIZABETH BERRY
> *Airedale and Welsh Terrier Rescue*

Both aging dogs and aging humans find it harder to deal with sudden changes in their daily life. Therefore, maintaining a routine for your terrier is one way to reduce its stress and increase its comfort level. You may need to hire someone to walk or feed your Welshie when you can't be there, but sticking to a schedule helps.

An old dog spends more time lying down and sleeping than a young dog. With that in mind, consider an orthopedic bed for your elderly pet. It can be more comfortable for arthritic joints than a regular dog bed. Some beds even have a heating element.

If your terrier is having accidents in its sleep, cover the bed with a washable and waterproof human bed pad. This will make clean-up easier.

A senior canine is less tolerant of extreme temperatures. It can't regulate its body temperature as well as it once did. So be vigilant that your dog stays cool in the summer and warm in the winter.

> **DID YOU KNOW?**
> **The Long Life of an Ancient Breed**
>
> Welsh Terriers are considered the oldest surviving dog breed in the United Kingdom, with a documented history that goes back centuries. The earliest surviving reference to the Welsh Terrier occurs in a poem written by a Welsh poet in 1450. The Welsh Terrier was first recognized by the AKC in 1888 when two of these black and tan dogs were registered with the AKC. These pioneering American canines were named T'Other and Which and were owned by Prescott Lawrence.

Make sure your old pet can move around the house safely. Pet steps or ramps can provide easy access to favorite places your terrier can no longer easily access on its own. Smooth floor surfaces like wood and tile are slippery for an old terrier, but carpeting and nonslip rugs can provide firm footing. Another option is to block access to areas your pet can no longer safely navigate.

It is especially important for an older Welshie to have secure footing where it stands to eat and drink. A nonslip mat by food and water dishes is a simple solution. I also like to elevate food and water dishes for elderly dogs. (A lowered head position while standing can stress joints.) Your terrier should be able to eat or drink without lowering its head or stretching its neck upward.

A dog that has lost some of its hearing may have trouble locating where a sound is coming from. The same thing can happen when a person experiences some hearing loss. So, you may need to help your old terrier find you when you call.

Sometimes owning an elderly Welshie seems like a lot of work. I've always felt my dogs give so much love and joy throughout their lives that giving them some comfort and joy in their final years is a worthwhile effort.

End of Life

> *Look for quality of life as your Welshie ages. Does it still have joy? There are few things more important to a Welsh than having a good time. Find the simple joys that your dog has always enjoyed and continue to do them. You may need to throw the ball a shorter distance or hide the toy in plain sight, but keep engaging the dog to be a Welsh until the very end. It doesn't matter how much wax is left; when the wick is gone, the candle burns out. Saying goodbye is the hardest decision you will ever make—and the greatest gift you will ever give.*
>
> ANNE PELLETIER
> *Bremadog Welsh*

Facing the loss of your pet is never easy. But when you have a terminally ill or frail senior dog, you may have time to plan for your dog's ending. You have the opportunity to make your Welshie's passing as easy and painless as possible. You also have choices to make.

Your vet should be able to suggest options for handling your dog's final exit. It may be possible to provide palliative care at home so that your dog dies pain-free in your home in its sleep. A vet may be able to visit your home to euthanize your ailing Welshie. Or you may prefer to have your dog euthanized at the vet's office. Take your time and make the choice that is right for you and your Welsh Terrier.

If you choose to euthanize your dog humanely, the hardest part may be deciding the right time. In my experience, it's not always easy to know when to say goodbye. If a dog is suffering greatly from illness or injury with no chance of recovery, the decision of when to put a pet to sleep is obvious. Unfortunately, when a dog experiences good days and bad days with its quality of life gradually decreasing, the right time for euthanasia may not be so clear-cut.

To choose the proper moment, it's important to know whether your dog's pain or other medical conditions can be controlled enough for it to be comfortable and enjoy life. A veterinarian can explain these issues and help you understand what difficulties your terrier may be facing in the future.

Also, consider other quality-of-life concerns, such as mobility, appetite, mental capacity, and comfort level. There are canine quality-of-life checklists available online that can help. Links for some of these sites are provided in Chapter 16. These checklists can be a useful tool, but in the end, you know your pet better than anyone else. The right choice may become clearer as you listen to your dog and talk to your vet as well as friends and family.

If you plan to have your dog die naturally at home, how will you make sure it remains pain-free? What will you do if your dog suddenly becomes extremely distressed? It's best to consider all the possible

Photo Courtesy of Krystle Sickman

Photo Courtesy of Jill Scott

scenarios so you can have backup plans just in case. Work with your vet to keep your dog as comfortable as possible. Many veterinary practices offer hospice care consultations and services. Some also make house calls.

If you choose to euthanize your dog, make sure you understand the process. Many veterinarians first sedate a dog before administering a drug to stop the dog's heart. Ask your vet how they handle euthanasia. It should be your choice whether or not to be there when it happens. If you are there, you should know what to expect.

You will also have to decide what to do with your beloved Welsh Terrier's body after death. Depending on where you live, you may be able to bury it at home. If that's not possible or not what you want, arrangements can be made for the body to be cremated and the ashes returned to you. (There is usually a choice of communal cremation or individual cremation.) A pet cemetery is another possibility. Your veterinarian's office should be able to provide information about cremation and pet cemeteries in your area. Some people don't want anything to do with the dead body once their pet's spirit has moved on, and in those cases, the veterinarian can dispose of it.

Grieving the Loss of Your Pet

It's normal to be upset and experience a range of emotions when your Welsh Terrier dies. Your house may seem empty and lonely, and certain times of day previously devoted to your dog may elicit extreme sadness. It's also not unusual to feel guilt and doubt about the decisions you made for your Welshie.

Chapter 15: The Senior Welsh Terrier

You've just lost your furry best friend or your furry child, so don't be ashamed of your grief. The staff at your veterinarian's office will understand, as will most dog-loving family members and friends. Don't listen to anyone who discourages your grieving or says that it was just a dog, so you should get over it.

Everyone mourns differently, and it's important to do what helps you with your grief. Creating a memorial for your terrier or holding a memorial service may be comforting. Or you may want to get another dog right away to ease your grief. This doesn't always help, especially if you expect the new dog to be just like your recently deceased pet.

Photo Courtesy of Martha Lisa Sagers

Talking about your former Welshie with friends and family may provide solace. There are even pet bereavement support groups to help grieving pet owners. Your vet's office may know of a local group. (See Chapter 16 for pet bereavement group resources.)

CHAPTER 16

Resources for Welsh Terrier Owners

Welsh Terrier Club of America https://welshterrier.org
(Contact the WTCA for information about regional Welsh Terrier clubs)

WTCARES https://welshterrierrescue.com/

American Kennel Club https://www.akc.org

AKC Purebred Alternative Listing Program https://www.akc.org/register/information/purebred-alternative-listing-pal/

Health

ASPCA Animal Poison Control (https://www.aspca.org/pet-care/animal-poison-control): 1-888-426-443

Pet Poison Helpline https://www.petpoisonhelpline.com: 1-855-764-7661

FDA Dangers for Pets Page https://www.fda.gov/animal-veterinary/animal-health-literacy/dangers-pets

Upright Canine Brigade provides information and support for canine megaesophagus caninemegaesophagusinfo.com

The Canine Epilepsy Network http://www.canine-epilepsy.net/

The Abbeyrose Foundation (founded by two Welsh Terrier breeders and a dog trainer) is dedicated to healthy pets and their people. Their

Chapter 16: Resources for Welsh Terrier Owners

Photo Courtesy of John Melair

work is rooted in science, research, and experience in applying a natural/holistic approach to living while not abandoning conventional approaches when appropriate. https://abbeyrosefoundation.org/

Orthopedic Foundation for Animals – The Canine Health Information Center https://ofa.org

End of Life

International Association for Animal Hospice and Palliative Care with a directory of In-Home Pet Hospice and Euthanasia Providers
https://iaahpc.org/find-support/

Association for Pet Loss and Bereavement
https://www.aplb.org/support/

Lap of Love is a nationwide network of veterinarians providing veterinary hospice and in-home euthanasia. The website also lists pet loss and grief counseling resources and quality of life assessment tools
https://www.lapoflove.com

Pet Loss Help https://petlosshelp.net

The Pet Loss Support Page https://www.pet-loss.net

Pet Loss Grief Support, Rainbow Bridge & Candle Ceremony https://www.petloss.com

Travel

Center for Pet Safety https://www.centerforpetsafety.org

International Air Transportation Association's Traveler's Pet Corner https://www.iata.org/en/programs/cargo/live-animals/pets/

The Ruthi Tag Tote https://www.ruthihome.com/

Pet First Aid by American Red Cross

Rover

Wag!

BringFido

Dog Tricks

AKC Trick Dog Program https://www.akc.org/sports/trick-dog/about-trick-dog/

Do More With Your Dog https://domorewithyourdog.com/DogTricks/

Earthdog and Ratting

American Working Terrier Association https://www.awta.org

AKC Earthdog https://www.akc.org/sports/earthdog/

Barn Hunt Association https://www.barnhunt.com

Chapter 16: Resources for Welsh Terrier Owners

North American Sporting Dog Association https://nasda.dog

Website on Working Terriers in America http://www.terrierman.com

Companion Dog Activities

AKC Canine Good Citizenship https://www.akc.org/products-services/training-programs/canine-good-citizen/

AKC Farm Dog https://www.akc.org/sports/herding/farm-dog-certified-test/

AKC Rally https://www.akc.org/sports/rally/

AKC Obedience https://www.akc.org/sports/obedience/

World Canine Freestyle Organization https://www.worldcaninefreestyle.org

Musical Dog Sport Association https://musicaldogsport.org

Canine Freestyle Federation Inc. https://canine-freestyle.org

Therapy Dogs International https://www.tdi-dog.org

Lure Coursing/Terrier Racing

AKC Coursing https://www.akc.org/sports/coursing/

Jack Russell Club of America https://www.therealjackrussell.com

Flyball

North American Flyball Association http://www.flyball.org

United States Flyball League International https://www.u-fli.com

Agility

AKC Agility https://www.akc.org/sports/agility/

United States Dog Agility Association Inc https://www.usdaa.com

North American Dog Agility Council https://www.nadac.com

Nose Work

AKC Tracking https://www.akc.org/sports/tracking/

AKC Scent Work https://www.akc.org/sports/akc-scent-work/

National Association of Canine Scent Work https://www.nacsw.net

Training

Come Click! Dog training with Lucy Bailey of WYSIWYG Welsh Terriers, offering private lessons by video conference and in person. Bailey has numerous training certifications and has been training dogs since 1965. https://come-click.com

Linda Brisbin, an agility trainer and competitor, is a trailblazer for Welsh Terriers in American agility. Linda@teamtrouble.info

Diane Bauman is a world-renowned canine expert, teacher and trainer. Bauman helps her students (humans and their dogs) understand what they are doing and enjoy doing it. Her website offers some free instructional material. www.dianebauman.com

Dog Potential Unleashed provides a different dimension in dog training, specializing in problem-solving for teams who need a little help finding their best communication style and offering online and in-person classes. Trainer Frankie Joiris has experience with many terrier breeds, including Welsh Terriers. https://dogpotentialunleashed.com/

One Mind Dogs teaches people how to see the world from a dog's point of view to help create better communication and build a stronger bond between humans and their dogs. www.oneminddogs.com

Books & Magazines

Breed Characteristics & History:
The Welsh Terrier Handbook by I. Morlais Thomas, published by Nicholson & Watson, 1959.

The Welsh Terrier Leads the Way by Bardi McLennan, published by Doral Publishing, 1998. (This is a gold mine of Welsh Terrier history.)

Terriers - Their Training, Working & Management by Various Authorities, edited by A. Croxton Smith, published by Vintage Dog Book, 2009.

The Terriers of England and Wales: Their History and Development by Bryan Cummins, published by Friesen Press, 2019.

The Welsh Terrier: A Complete Anthology of the Dog by Various Authors, published by Vintage Dog Books, 2011.

Care:
Good Old Dog: Expert Advice for Keeping Your Aging Dog Happy, Healthy, and Comfortable by Faculty of the Cummings School of Veterinary Medicine at Tufts University, Nicholas H. Dodman (Editor), published by Mariner Books, 2010.

Grooming the Broken-Coated Terrier by Arden Ross, illustrations by Lori Bush. (Originally in Terrier Type) Available from the Airedale Club of America https://airedale.org/shopping/brochures-newsletter/grooming-the-broken-coated-terrier/

Mental Exercise for Dogs: The Best Dog Games for Improving Behavior, Strengthening the Bond, and Having Fun Together – Benefits for Both You and Your Furry Friend by Charlotte Nelson, published in 2023, available on Amazon.

Children's Books:
The Barker Twin series by Tomie dePaola is a series of nine children's books. The main characters are Welsh Terriers based on author dePaola's own Welsh Terriers.

A Clem Book series by Beatrice Phillpotts is a series of four childrens books featuring a Welsh Terrier named Clem. Published by George Weidenfeld & Nicholson, Ltd., 1987.

Earthdogs & Working/Hunting Terriers
Earthdog Ins and Outs, 2nd Edition by Jo Ann Frier-Murza, published by VGF Publications, 2010. (The best book on den trials for Earthdogs that will ever be written.)

Sport With Terriers by Patricia Adams Lent (AWTA founder), published by Arner Publications, 1973.

Hunt And Working Terriers by Jocelyn Lucas, originally published in 1931. Published in 2010 by Vintage Dog Books.

The Sporting Terrier by D. Brian Plummer, published by Boydell Press, 1992.

The Working Terrier by D. Brian Plummer, published by Boydell Press, 1978.

Tales of a Rat-Hunting Man by D. Brian Plummer, published by Boydell Press, 1978.

Training:
Dog Smart: Evidence-based Training with The Science Dog by Linda Case, published by AutumnGold Publishing, 2018.

Crate Games for Motivation and Control by Susan Garrett
DVD: https://dogsthat.com/product/crate-games/
Crate Games Online: https://dogsthat.com/product/crategames-online/

Chapter 16: Resources for Welsh Terrier Owners

Love Has No Age Limit: Welcoming an Adopted Dog into Your Home by Patricia McConnell and Karen London, published by McConnell Publishing, 2011.

The Other End of Leash: Why We Do What We Do Around Dogs, by Patricia McConnell, published by Random House, 2002.

Way to Go! How to Housetrain a Dog of Any Age, by Karen B. London and Patricia McConnell, published by Dog's Best Friend, 2003.

Reaching the Animal Mind by Karen Pryor, published by Scribner, 2010.

Clicking with Your Dog: Step-by-Step in Pictures by Peggy Tillman, published by Sunshine Books, 2006.

Fired Up, Frantic and Freaked Out: Training Crazy Dogs from Over the Top to Under Control by Laura VanArendonk Baugh, published by Aeclipse Press, 2013.

Social, Civil and Savvy: Training and Socializing Puppies to Become the Best Dogs Possible by Laura VanArendonk Baugh, published by Aeclipse Press, 2017.

Perfect Puppy in 7 Days by Sophia Yin, published by CattleDog Publishing, 2011.

Agility:

Dog Agility: Start to Finish, an interactive ebook (available at www.dianebauman.com) by Diane Bauman and Jessica Ajoux, over 75 minutes of linked training videos, information is updated as sport evolves, 2008.

Clean Run Magazine is a monthly magazine for dog agility enthusiasts. https://www.cleanrun.com

www.ingramcontent.com/pod-product-compliance
Lightning Source LLC
Chambersburg PA
CBHW050728010526
44107CB00009B/785